Almere Architecture City

Ans van Berkum, **Odette Breijinck**
photography: Hans Jan Dürr, Geert van der Wijk

nai010 publishers

Welcome to Almere

Almere is now almost 50 years old and presents itself as one of the most daring building projects in the history of the Netherlands. Everything had to be reinvented here as the city arose on the largest ship graveyard of our country: the pristine bottom of the Zuiderzee. This practical guide presents Almere by looking at 100 building projects that highlight the development of this brand-new city in the empty polder landscape. Internationally renowned architects such as Rem Koolhaas and Christian de Portzamparc make an appearance, as are numerous Dutch firms that accepted unparalleled challenges. After all, the aim was to develop a varied urban landscape in which the latest in residential architecture would always prevail.

No wonder that Almere became the leader in DIY construction. It started with experiments such as De Fantasie and De Realiteit. The next step was Wild Living and Wanted Living, where future residents could present their wishes to developers. Steps were taken with private and collective commissioning in the Overgooi, Noorderplassen and Poort neighbourhoods. For now, this development ends in Oosterwold, where the creativity of a large number of people is allowed to flourish in all phases of the building process.

This guide tells the tale of remarkable places, daring actions, and inevitable setbacks. It includes tips on where to find good café's, cultural gems, and B&Bs. Almere: architecture city in nature.

Content

The Multi-Core City

This design is the secret of Almere and a treasure worth cherishing

Hans Warrink

Almere was developed as composition of cores of varying sizes in a vast urban landscape, based on the garden city concept of Ebenezer Howard (1850-1928). This socially committed journalist came up with an alternative for the polluted English industrial cities: smoky slums where people could hardly breathe. Garden cities combine the benefits of the fresh countryside with the opportunities of the city. They consist of individual city districts, surrounded by water and green. The people reside there in bright houses and breathe clean air, but also have jobs and leisure time.

The landscape designated for this construction was first laid out. Fifty years of growing power later, the city is surrounded with a wealth of woodlands and water. Gradually, its six cores took shape there. The centre of Almere Haven 57 became a modern version of a Zuiderzee town, surrounded by child-friendly residential neighbourhoods with much water and greenery. Almere Stad, the future heart of the city, was to have a more urban look 19 with many straight lines, broad avenues, city parks, and the city centre with high-rises 11. Almere Buiten's layout was related to the coarse grid of polder parcellation. Here, business districts were developed first, before the residential quarters.

Stedenwijk, Almere Stad, 1979

The Evenaar with its green central reservation became the axis of this city district. Originally, Almere Poort's theme was to be sports, but in the end 'urbanity' was chosen as its profile, with a core area for private and collective commissions.

All the neighbourhoods look different and at times one may see a house that raises some people's eyebrows. Almere Duin, built as a very urban beach town in the southwest part of Almere Poort, forms the bridge with its sister city Amsterdam. Almere Hout started with many villas in parklike greenery, but with the Oosterwold neighbourhood it became a pinnacle of DIY building. And Almere Pampus may become quite dense around the planned Metro station on the Almere-Amsterdam line, but its atmosphere remains defined by the abundance of water and woodlands already there. The construction of this IJmeer connection remains a precondition for the Almere municipality for starting to build this neighbourhood.

Many people highly value the multi-core structure of Almere. However, this layout is by no means definitive as yet. The desire for liveliness and more metropolitan services as well as the plans to build another 10,000 to 15,000 houses in Almere Stad may pose a threat to the original concept. At the moment Almere has five municipal monuments. It would be well worth considering adding the multi-core structure to this lineup, being an exceptional and by now historic quality of Almere.

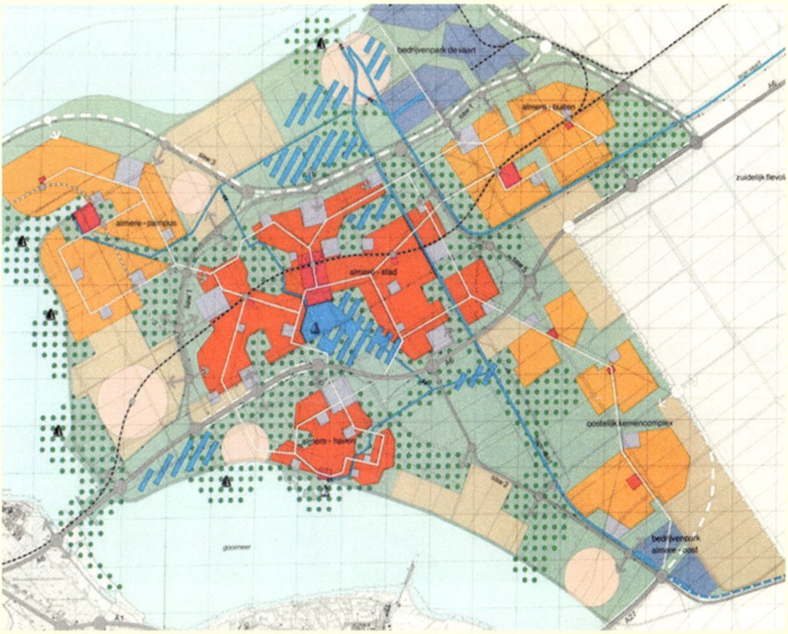

Design Structure Plan Almere, 1977

1 NS Station Almere Centrum

Stationsplein
Peter Kilsdonk
1983-1987

Rail travellers arriving in Almere will first of all experience the special construction of the station's roof. It consists of a web of signal red steel, a so-called 'spaceframe'. It is a construction of steel girders connected by tubes that come together at nodes; a system that allows large spans. Square skylights were cut out in the overhead roof. The lifts and stairways have red accents. On the outside one sees blue steel beams that have an independent bearing function. A series of green lamps are hung in a longitudinal direction, forming a straight line when seen from a certain position. In the high station hall and at the entrances the roof is supported by red, open steel constructions that rest on black columns with a single point. The angularly protruding skylights there connect the front and back facades. They continue above the entrances in protruding windows that are shaped like little houses. These prominent facades, which keep the spaceframe in sight, make up the light but still monumental look of this station. The architectural school applied here by Kilsdonk is called 'High Tech'. It is an optimistic form language in primary colours that he also applied in Zaandam, Duivendrecht and Lelystad Centrum.

Hello Catering

In 2023, Station Square underwent a metamorphosis. The office buildings on both sides of the main entrance of the train station were transformed into multifunctional buildings with many bars and restaurants in the plinth, with apartments over them. The facades of both office buildings were given to extra floors to accommodate these. This was a sustainable solution as the existing framework and foundation could be reused. The dark grey facades did lend a touch of style to the station building. This project by Paul de Ruiter was nominated for the Almere Architectural Award in 2024.

2 Mandelapark

Mandelaplein
Karres+Brands
2006-2011
Bart Brands, Jeroen Marseille, Joost de Natris, Paul Portheine, Uta Krause, Carlie Young, Annalen Grüss (proj.)
Dam and Partners, ZZDP, Cie Architects (collaborators)

On the northside of train station Almere Centrum 1 lies Mandelapark, made up of ponds, grasses, perennial plants and flowering shrubs. It is hidden behind three giant office buildings, the highest of which stands at 120 metres. It's an oasis, stretching out over two 4-tier underground parking garages with 505 spots and connecting the business centre with the residential Staatslieden neighbourhood. This 200-metre green strip provides openness to the otherwise urban environment. From a bird's eye view, the ground plan resembles an enlarged microscopic culture on a petri dish of organic forms that change colour with the seasons.
The glass entry points, embedded in the park as follies, join in this form language. A band of grown-up sycamores encircles the park, delineating it both visually and spatially.
The footpaths going through the park are made of terrazzo asphalt. It playfully interacts with the natural stone pavement of the square directly behind the station, which coincides with the paving in the Mandelapark like a barcode. This park is one of the largest roof parks in the Netherlands and is part of the masterplan 11, designed by Rem Koolhaas in 1994. The park added an 'instant identity' to the 'instant skyline'.

Memorial to Slavery

On 30 June 2023, the almost two metre high, bronze Memorial to Slavery by Almerian artist Patrick Mezas was given a prominent place in the Mandelapark. It depicts an enslaved man, still with a chain around his ankle, holding up a baby. This child symbolises Almere as a young city. The man is surrounded by symbols that refer to buildings in the Netherlands that are related to slavery. The placing of the statue was an important moment for the large community of people of Surinam origin in Almere.

3 Carlton

P.J. Oudweg 4
Dam & Partners
2007-2010
Diederik Dam (proj.)
Karres+Brands (landscape)

Behind Station Almere Centrum 1 lies the office complex Almere l'Hermitage, made up of the Carlton Tower (World Trade Centre) and two other buildings. At 120 metres, the Carlton is the highest building in the city, making it an important point of orientation. Most prominent are the flame-red vertical aluminium ribs decorating the glass facades in various patterns. Higher up, the pattern becomes more transparent. The building stands on a platelike base and consists of three volumes: a high central part with 32 floors, flanked by two lower volumes of six and twelve floors, respectively. The entrance at Busplein has tall, slender white columns, the entrance at P.J. Oudweg 4 has low, black columns. The plinth accommodates bars, restaurants, and shops. By regarding the building with its rectangular base form and great height as facade architecture, it functions as a logical boundary behind which the city centre reveals itself. The Carlton houses the WTC, which used to be located at the Alnovum (P.J. Oudweg 1) designed by Benthem Crouwel Architects in 1999.

Dark side

The drawback to the zest for growth and transformation in cities, and Almere is no exception, is the displacement of artworks in public space: art often being the victim. The Bezinningsmonument (Reflection Monument) (1992) by Jan van IJzendoorn, an ellipse on a black pedestal, had been placed on a marble plateau in Mandela square. It was unceremoniously moved for a second time to a place two hundred metres away at Landdrostdreef. Gone is the pedestal, gone is the maxim, gone is the surrounding space needed for reflection.

4 Martinez

Mandelaplein 1
ZZDP Architecten
2010-2017

The Martinez office tower, a beacon of modernist architecture, was completed in 2011, in the middle of the construction crisis the Netherlands were facing at the time. With its height of seventy metres, the tower rose up as a symbol of ambition and progress, but because of the crisis it stood empty for a long time. In 2017 the tower got a new lease on life when it was transformed from an office building into a more versatile and dynamic complex. In view of the growing importance of multifunctional spaces in modern urban centres the tower was converted into a hotel with 158 rooms, a luxurious spa and exclusive business club, complete with a panoramic terrace on the fifteenth floor.
The building is slender and airy because of its height and the use of transparent and green glass. The meandering facade allows plenty of daylight to enter. The four linked flat discs of glass and steel come together in a central core. The airy character is reinforced by the fact that not all disks extend to the ground but protrude on either the second or fourth floor. The plinth houses bars and restaurants. The design brings a little of the Amsterdam Zuidas to Almere.

Highest?

In Almere, the highest building is the Carlton (2010) at 120 metres, followed by the Euro Tower (2004) at 80 metres. The Martinez proudly takes third place at 78 metres. The realisation of the skyline – with an average height of 70 metres – and the business district of Almere makes for interesting images with cranes as the protagonists.

5 La Défense

W. Dreesweg
UN Studio
1999-2004
Ben van Berkel (proj.)

The multitenant business centre La Défense is situated in a small-scale office park and consists of two building volumes that envelop two spacious inner courtyards. On the outer edge, along the avenue and smaller streets, the facades are clad in studded aluminium sheets. This exterior sharply contrasts with the lively interior walls, where a special foil in the glass provides a dynamic play of light. The integration with the urban plan was carefully prepared and executed. The height of the exterior facades and the intimate inner courtyards fit well within the environment. The exterior walls speak to the urban context, whereas the interior walls were designed with the users in mind. The unique atmosphere of the inner courtyard with its enchanting colours creates a pleasant environment for the building's users. This tranquil ambience will surely benefit the third round of residents after the renovation. Following the Tax Authority, the employee insurance agency UWV had offices here. In 2025, the space will be allocated to holders of residence permits, who will make their homes in the converted offices. In 2013, two companion sculptures by Ram Katzir, *Where Thoughts Are* were installed, lending an element of style to the inner courtyard.

Rainbow

The glass facades of the interior courtyard are clad with a foil produced by 3M that reflects in bright red, yellow, and green. The facades' colour changes with one's position and/or that of the sun. 3M had originally developed this Radiant Light Film for a perfume bottle. While that didn't work out, it became a real eyecatcher with this building.

6 Tarra Tower

Busplein 26-40
MVRDV
1999-2002
Winy Maas (proj.)

Tarra is the difference between gross and net, the expendable part. In this case it is the construction, which is on the outside of the building. At Tarra Tower it is a load bearing, 60 cm thick concrete harness, articulated by a rigid grid of horizontal grooves. The nine office floors are hidden behind it. This charcoal grey skeleton covers the facades from bottom to top, only sparingly interrupted by openings that are three times the size of the default module. Because of the prominent material and rhythm, the building exudes both robustness and calm. The expressive walls with their deep reveals create a functional distance between the inner world of the offices and the busy street life. In this mega Jenga tower the corners are kept 'free' by the special load-bearing structure, which also makes the building look slender and slim.
The freestanding structure lies opposite the train station 1, directly by the bus station, a bicycle path, and the street: an infrastructure node where each mode of transport has its own place.
In 2003, architect Winy Maas' design for the Tarra Tower was nominated for the Almere Architecture Award.

Impact

Tarra Tower is one of the first designs for Almere by MVRDV, an acronym of the last names of architects Winy Maas, Jacob van Rijs and Nathalie de Vries. MVRDV won several commissions from the municipality and has left its mark on the city. They also developed the structure vision 2030, a conceptual vision to guide the growth of the city. Just like The Landscape of Alternatives, Oosterwold, and the design for the Floriade with its arboretum, all unique urban experiments befitting the architectural history of Almere.

7 ANNO

Grote Markt 121
Jo Coenen
1983-1988

At Grote Markt, the ANNO building stands out with its prominent form language that is reminiscent of the 1950s. Originally designed as a Grand Café and hotel, it extends across three stories, laid out around a spectacular atrium. ANNO is now all about dining, drinking, dancing, and overnight accommodation. The original Pizza Point has been replaced with a kitchen that serves dishes from all over the world.
The facade is made of bricks in two colours, sand and beige, in horizontal courses. On the south side the bricks stick out more and more going up, creating an overhang that provides shelter for the balconies of the hotel rooms. The high atrium is a bold statement and skylights guarantee enough daylight coming in. The storey-high glass facades have been subtly placed slightly inwards.
In consultation with Geert Coenen a number of changes have been made to the Costco since then: the former company residence was added to the hotel; the stairwell and the void leading to the mezzanine were enlarged. A large aluminium shaft stands like a guard in the brick outer wall, next to a glass cube for smokers, added later. This project has won several prizes, including the prestigious Nai Architecture Award.

Goodbye stage

A mobile stage once stood on the Grote Markt like a giant crane. This meant that parking space had to make way for outdoor cafés. In 1999, Michael van Gessel redesigned the square, including this movable stage. Trees were rearranged into small groups allowing huge crowds to enjoy performances on national holidays. Only belatedly the realisation came that this idea also had its drawbacks: the noise generated by big events led to protests and, eventually, to the stage being demolished.

8 Town Hall

Stadhuisplein 1
Dam & Partners
1984-1986
Cees Dam (proj.); Diederik Dam
(exp. 2004-2005)

The building consists of two wings of five storeys, perpendicular to each other and parallel to two streets. It wasn't until 2005 that a third wing, reaching a height of ten storeys, was added between the original two wings. The glass wing housing the municipal administration, elegantly curves around this third wing, and is known as 'the banana'. The impressive hall, where the three main volumes meet, also functions as a passage to Stadhuisplein from the parking lot behind the buildings.
The building radiates allure from various dramatic elements, such as the majestic stairways that cut through the two outer wings and are clad in flame-red studded lino, lit by an elongated skylight. The restrooms have white tiles decorated with golden circles and the letters C and D of Cees Dam. In some places, also on the outside facades, glass mosaic with a golden shine has been applied.
The concrete facades have a classic layout in three courses: a concrete base, a marble middle part and a cornice, articulated by round recess. The impressive, circular council chamber at the side of the square is suspended above the entrance. A covered passage of steel and glass forms the axis between the front and the back, where we find the wedding room.

Glass Palace?

Cees Dam was commissioned to design City Hall, after his plan for a modernist 'glass palace' for Almere Haven presented in March 1977 had not been approved by the then ZIJP (a public government body that preceded the municipality).
It was supposed to have been built on a lot behind Corrosia 60, near secondary school De Meergronden. The design met with resistance from residents and was never realised.

9 The New Library

Stadhuisplein 101
Meyer & Van Schooten
2005-2009
Barry van Waveren (proj.)

Designed as a monolith, The New Library distinguishes itself with concrete elements with a horizontal relief and a front that is placed slightly outwards. Meyer & Van Schooten designed this building on a triangular lot with an upward sloping surface level to which the library adapts itself. The concrete elements with glistening basalt particles give the building a distinguished look, befitting a temple of culture. The entrance with escalators is very inviting, guiding visitors to the central hall where spacious voids create a hospitable and uncluttered atmosphere. Horizontal strip windows let in ample daylight. The offices are on the first and third floor.

The glass facades provide contact with the outside world everywhere. Energy-saving escalators that accelerate when visitors step onto them, provide access to the book collection, which is appealingly displayed on large plateaus. A serene, enclosed garden compensates for the lack of greenery in the surroundings. On the fourth floor are cabins for studying and large tables with hookups for laptops. A café and two film rooms on the first and second floor contribute to the versatility of the building, which, thanks to connecting sight lines, radiates an atmosphere of openness. Here, people can read, study, relax and experience the city around them. If the architects could be criticised for one thing, it would be that the entrance is not very inviting. People have to make the effort to come in and obtain a sense of the atmosphere.

LOLA

On Stadhuispromenade, between The New Library and City Hall 8, lies a newly laid-out city park (2019-2022). It is a result of the Floriade 26 and part of the Groene Loper (Green Carpet), which runs from the station to the Weerwater. Stones were replaced by greenery. In wadis and along the edge native plants and trees were planted. A clever gutter system catches rainwater. In the middle a colourful bench undulates, the longest bench in Almere. The design is by LOLA Landscape, who allowed input by residents. It is taken full advantage of by both the young and the old.

10 HIGHnote

Landdrostdreef
Studioninedots
2022-2023

Driving towards HIGHnote from Cinemadreef, this landmark functions as the entrance to the city centre. With its back to Landdrostdreef, its four storeys descend like a staircase in the direction of the centre. Embedded in the inner-city fabric on a former triangular parking lot, the building is a striking apparition: it is the first residential high-rise in the city centre. The design provides for publicly accessible spaces on the ground floor for catering and retail. Along the edge of the lot a single continuous peristyle of bold columns borders these public spaces. Higher up, 157 rental apartments for starters in the housing market have been realised in staggered blocks. The pink facades are made of prefabricated concrete. The square building elements, from the peristyle to windows and balconies, create a pleasant rhythm.
This residential concept is new to Almere. The size of the apartments varies between 45 and 70 m^2. The 67 'Friends apartments', where people live together but have individual leases, measure between 65 and 100 m^2.
In addition, HIGHnote offers flexibility in the spatial design and programming. This means that the apartments can be adapted or combined at a later stage. This adaptive quality makes the building sustainable and future proof.

Welcome to Almere

I remember vividly that first Friday afternoon that me and my wife came down here to take a look. I wasn't pleased at all, really. Such cold, barren, grey buildings.

Harsh words indeed by journalist and troubadour Henk Kruit, a well-known but critical Almerian from the early days. An outspoken but soft-hearted man, he devoted himself to the cause of Rumanian orphans and, among other things, organised the Jazz Below the Sea festival. After 25 years of this he was awarded the Bonifatius Pin. During a performance he became unwell and died shortly after at the age of 56.

11 Elevated Ground Level

Citadel
OMA
1994-2010
Rem Koolhaas, Floris Alkemade (proj.), DS landschapsarchitecten (landscape)

Planning Almere's new city centre gained urgency after 1990, as the cores Haven, Stad, and Buiten began to function as separate units. A new city centre would restore the cohesion. Following a tender procedure, the commission was given to Rem Koolhaas' Office for Metropolitan Architecture (OMA). They had won the tender with a master plan that implemented an urban core of 800 × 800 metres within the existing city centre with facilities at the level of a city with a population of 180,000. The programme combines working, living, shopping, culture, leisure, and sports into an attractive mix.
OMA convinced the municipality with the design that broke through the existing grid structure in two ways. First, the ground level was heightened by nine metres, making the city's heart rise above the polder plane in a spectacular fashion. In addition, the grid was given a 'kink' and the straight-lined streets were augmented with diagonal sightlines. The street pattern and the difference in height provide visitors with exciting vistas. This urban iconography represents the modernist, avant-gardist, and progressive qualities that Almere as a young city wants to exude.

11a The Citadel

Citadel
Christian de Portzamparc
2004-2006

At the top is the Citadel: French architect Christian de Portzamparc drew inspiration from town castles. Two crossing pedestrian streets divide the complex into four quadrants with shops on the ground floor and apartments over them. The cantilevered concrete course has an irregular horizontal relief, representing the layers of earth deep below the passers-by. Like a 'magic carpet', nature has been moved to the upper storey where the sloping lawn refers to the commons that traditionally made up the centre of villages. At the edges of this green carpet De Portzamparc situated terraced houses with flat roofs that alternate in depth, width, and height.
At the centre of this ensemble stands a tower of six storeys, with one apartment on each floor and separate lifts to each apartment. This 'donjon' completes the ensemble.

12 Urban Entertainment Centre

Brouwerstraat/Koetsierbaan
Alsop Architects
1998-2004
William Alsop (proj.)

The project consists of a collection of objects that are stylistically different on purpose, making for a welcome variety. The four-storey hotel with 117 rooms is clad in hardwood. The horizontal fenestration marks the floors in the oblique facades. The blob-like protuberance is the entrance to the café-restaurant. This blob is clad in copper and has one side in yellow on the service road, evoking associations with a sliced potato in a brown peel. Further down is a large blob of zinc, a concert hall for pop music. The muted zinc has a structure of vertical strokes, lending allure to the robust form. The thick walls provide perfect sound insulation. This thickness can be seen at the scarce, deep openings.

12a Schipperplein

Koetsierbaan
DS Landschapsarchitecten
2004-2008
Marseille Buiten (Redevelopment 2013)

One level down lies a small sunken square. When the original design of 2004 no longer met the needs, it was transformed in 2013 into a green oasis, an inviting, undulating landscape. New ornamental plants in elevated borders enclose a pond/ice-skating rink inlaid with new bamboo boardwalks. In summer a green jewel, in winter a fun ice rink.

The rectangular shop next to the music hall faces the street with a coloured-glass facade, in harmony with the brand logos of the electronic devices sold here. The transparent overhang creates a sense of security at street level. Across from the shop is an activity centre with a facade that is made up of a pink surface and a glass section. At one time, a bowling alley and a bar were there. The narrow windows in the pink surface lend the facade a sleek and graphic look. The back of the building is clad in patinated copper.
The glass box of the activity centre has oblique rebates, also a feature of the restaurant section higher up, which has a finish of brown strips. A bicycle parking with a suspended roof and a small office building clad in red tiles complete the ensemble.

13 Kunstlinie

Esplanade 10
SANAA
2004-2006
Kazuyo Sejima, Ryue Nishizawa (proj.); Oscar Vos (KRFT) (exp. 2016)

On the Weerwater lake lies De Kunstlinie, a building with a ground plan of 100 × 100 metres. Three rectangular hall volumes rise from this base. Behind the small hall is the exhibition wing with seven daylight rooms, a function that was added in 2016. The mid-sized and large halls rise up firmly into the sky.
The spacious entrance hall accommodates a reception area, catering, ticket sales, and the museum shop. Only the theatre lobby is high (25 metres) providing room for an enormous mural by Michael Lin, inspired by a Vlisco fabric. At the loading and unloading side of the building is a bright white spiral, visible from the outside. This spiral staircase, finished with a steel wall, brings visitors to the upper floor. Via the landing, an overhead glass bridge leads to the offices.
On the ground floor, SANAA created 'a city within a city'. It consists of a sequence of white rooms, hallways, patios, and inner courtyards with many vistas. The steel load bearing construction is connected to the glass facades in an ingenious manner, necessitating just a minimum number of columns to support the entire structure. The lightness of the construction is in line with the atmosphere of the place, emphasising its architectural beauty.

Haiku

In the floor of the main hall a memorial stone with a Japanese haiku was placed.

water glass and light –
a monument to dreaming –
in a new city

14 The Wave

Koetsierbaan
René van Zuuk
2003-2004

A particular building volume on the waterfront that immediately catches the eye is the residential complex The Wave, with 49 spacious owner-occupied apartments in four variations. The apartments are distributed across six floors. The scaled facades of the expressive building are made up of coated aluminium parts. The cavities and protrusions in the facade all have a functional basis. The dent on the north side marks the entrance, while the bulging in the south facade was created by adding patios to some of the apartments. On the waterfront this billowing is the strongest, casting a shadow in the form of a wave. It makes the facade reflect the ever-moving water at its foot.
Van Zuuk has realised a sturdy form with a horizontal silhouette as a counterpoint to the adjacent high-rise buildings. The design of The Wave is based on analysis of the formwork construction for tunnels. The concrete framework becomes dynamic through variations in length, which creates the waveform. The block stands out in the urban landscape and functions as a landmark at the entrance to the west side of the city. It fuses into the glass residential towers nearby. This project shows that ingenious construction and aesthetical design go together well.

Photogenic

In the 1990s, social housing on Schipperkade had to make way for the new heart of the city. The skyline that replaced it characterises Almere with prominent buildings such as Silverline, The Wave, Side by Side and Kunstlinie. High-rise construction transformed commuter town Almere into a modern city.

15 De Smaragd (The Emerald)

De Diagonaal
Gigon Guyer Architects
2004-2007
Annette Gigon (proj.)

To motorists on Hospitaaldreef roundabout, De Smaragd (The Emerald) is a striking beacon at the entrance of the tunnel leading to the city centre. This is because it is the only building with eye-catching colours. Its slanting walls guarantee optimum light incidence. On the first two floors is a department store with eight residential layers above it. These have zigzagging balconies all-around, reminiscent of the cut facets of a precious stone: the emerald. Higher up, the form changes and the volume increases, giving the building a dynamic look. De Smaragd's colour concept was developed in collaboration with the Swiss artist Adrian Schiess. The orange on the southwest side stands out in particular. In addition to the striking colours, the cantilevered facades are quite special. This building for living and shopping is situated on the highest point of the curved surface level with access roads to the 'underworld' of amenities and infrastructure underneath. At the higher car-free shopping area the reflection of light on the glass walls creates the illusion of a wider street, making the whole complex even more impressive. De Smaragd is a truly remarkable building in the urban landscape.

Walk of Fame

In the city centre special tiles are placed here and there in the pavement of Chinese granite. This is the 'Walk of Fame Almere' – a route of dozens of tiles in the centre that tell the story of the city. Each tile highlights a meaningful event, development, or an important person in a certain year. A QR code on the tiles provides access to more background information. Every year the citizens of Almere vote on who or what the next tile will be dedicated to.

16 Lakeside

Forum
SeARCH
2005-2007
Bjarne Mastenbroek (proj.)

Like a transformer with a twisted base, this reticular block is situated on the edge of the Esplanade. The striking trapezium-shaped substructure forms the base for the rectangular apartment block. The twisted tower and obliquely sloping substructure make this into a special high-rise. The volumes of the substructure and upper structure are 'morphed' together with a twisted connecting-piece. Glass and aluminium panels are also twisted where needed. All around the facade are strongly recessed loggias, which contribute to good climate control inside the apartments. The grey panels that fence in the loggias have patterns reminiscent of crocheted curtains.
In the plinth, which also houses a bar and restaurant, the massive supports of the tower have been purposefully left in view.
The twisting of the building was applied in order to maintain the sightline from the highest point of the surface level, the Diagonaal, to the Weerwater lake 24. This is one of the qualities added to the city centre by OMA to introduce better dynamics and more excitement to the shopping area. The combination of form, materials, and functionality makes the Lakeside an iconic part of the urban environment.

Flaw

A 'flaw' in the development of the city centre is wind nuisance. To tackle this problem, large transparent wind awnings were installed in 2013 in several places such as the Forum and De Diagonaal. On Belfortplein windbreaks were placed for the same reason. These adjustments, fitted with LED lights, are designed to improve the atmosphere and character of the heart of the city. In addition, landscape architects from Copijn were employed to raise the granite, create cosy corners, and plant trees, all of which contributes to a more pleasant and greener environment.

17 Kinepolis Cinema

Forum
OMA
2002-2005
Floris Alkemade (proj.)

Prominently situated on the Forum, where various pedestrian routes meet, is a large rectangular box that houses the cinema. When the lights go on at night, the building appears to hover and to free itself from its surroundings. The large building block has a dark glass plinth whereas the closed-off part is clad in gauze-like sheet material. The building sits on huge concrete columns.
The eight cinema theatres, with a combined capacity of 2100 seats, are suspended from the roof construction in an inventive manner. In addition to regular seats, six of the theatres have so-called 'cosy seats' that provide extra space and privacy so that visitors can enjoy the film within their own bubble.
The large entrance hall has a mega staircase that rolls down like a waterfall. The huge, carpeted steps make for a warm welcome. There is a theatrical feel here as if one is on one's way to a premiere. Various refreshment stalls and kiosks mark the route towards a spacious foyer where tickets can be bought. In the continuous plinth are spaces for various commercial functions. Below ground, via the parking garage, the building is connected to the orange-brown residential building of Van Sambeek and Van Veen Architecten.

Pi

With a single, large, irregular rift Petra Blaisse's Swamp Garden creates an open 'wound' from which water, wet soil, and trees appear. Along the edges concrete pegs point diagonally upwards. Swamp trees grow through the open roof. Special light effects light up treetops or create shifting shadows. The number Pi, written in giant numbers on the footpath, as a symbol for the unending task posed by urbanisation.

18 Esplanade

Esplanade 10
Echo Urban Design
2017-2018
Robbert Jan van der Veen (proj.)

In the 'eternally young inner city of Almere', seven squares were created as attractive places for events and relaxation. The biggest of these is the Esplanade and its holiday atmosphere is enhanced by its location on the Weerwater lake 24 with its beach – which has a Romney hut as a beach bar – expansive lawns that invite picnics, and a challenging water element with height differences. This is the third layout of the square, since the dusty top layer, like the one in the Jardin du Luxembourg in Paris, was removed and replaced by asphalt in a light pink colour in 2011. Echo Urban Design transformed the enormous expanse of concrete into a public space that invites gatherings. To achieve this, they made use of the existing layers and height differences of the square in creating a terrace-shaped landscape. The differences in height were given extra emphasis by placing elegant white benches between the borders. The scattered green lawns welcome relaxation and play. The parklike square counterbalances the urban atmosphere by creating a positive, open space. The broad, paved footpaths, which cut through the green organically like a pretzel, safeguard the access of emergency services. The square easily accommodates 20,000 people. From here one can 'climb' the raised surface level.

Puffin

In 2023, a remarkable work of art was installed on the lift building at the level of the stairs of the Kunstlinie, across from the hotel. It is a puffin, brightening up the surroundings. The lift shaft was also given a facelift with bands of blue, and now has this cartoon character on top. Street Art Frankey could not have come up with a better symbol to portray Almere. The puffin in red, yellow, and blue, is Frankey's first artwork in Almere. A drawn cartoon figure for the city of the drawing board.

19 De Zoetelaar

Zoetelaar Passage
Kees Rijnboutt, Ben Loerakker
1979-1981
Bakker & Verhoeff (exp. 1983-1985)

The designers of Almere were of the opinion that historical references would give people a sense of home. In line with this view, architect Kees Rijnboutt proposed a shopping arcade. Arcades were first built by the end of the nineteenth century when the need arose for shops selling the luxury consumer items that were beginning to flood the market. In the city centres of cities such as The Hague, Paris, and Brussels covered streets appeared, as a transition between the public nature of city streets and a more domestic atmosphere. No intimacy and dimly lit premises with luxury items for the rich here, but openness, freshness, and a low-threshold variety of goods. The slender vertical articulation of the outside facades in orange-brown brick is reminiscent of classical architecture. The interior was painted yellow and light blue, a style characteristic of postmodernism. That original arcade with its half-round glass cover was pretty, but not very practical. Especially the acoustics were a problem. Renovation was quick to come, and the pastel hues had to make way for new, fashionable colours. Owners and managers of shops and offices may come and go, but De Zoetelaar remains a nice, sheltered place where the shoppers are indeed at home.

Off You Go!

Museum De Paviljoens by Hilde Daem and Paul Robbrecht formed a remarkable ensemble in the heart of the city in the form of railway cars that were brought here from the German city of Kassel in 1994. There, they were used as an exhibition site for the 9th Documenta, an important international art event. They were allowed to have the same purpose in Almere until 2013, but then it was 'off you go'. Rumour has it that they were sold for a mere 50,000 euros to the city of Amersfoort, where they were installed in the effervescent Oliemolenkwartier neighbourhood. Talk about missed opportunities...

20 Flevoziekenhuis (Hospital)

Hospitaalweg 1
Campman Tennekes De Jong;
Wiegerinck Architecten
1991-2005; 2010
Jan Tennekes (proj.)

The Flevoziekenhuis (hospital) stands out with its large, oval-shaped low-rise building that one does not immediately associate with a modern, high-tech hospital. With this brick building Almere wanted to bring back the old-fashioned 'guest house' function, with space for social encounters in addition to medical services. The first phase of the Flevoziekenhuis was opened in 1991 and at the time it was still a provincial hospital in rural surroundings. The second phase was completed in 2010 and gave the building a more urban status. The restrained design and embeddedness within the surroundings make for a natural connection with the new city centre. The originally white building features an impressive glass roof construction that connects the various wards like a gallery. The younger chestnut brick building embraces the older one. The facade has a strongly horizontal articulation with rounded corners. The windows, which are continuous across the entire facade, stress the horizontal appearance, as does the jointing, which was done horizontally with a deep-lying horizontal joint. This alternates with vertical expansion joints. The main hall, laid out as a square with shops and a café-restaurant, invites people to meet there, making it a true 'guest house'.
The hospital has extensive facilities for rehabilitation and separate entrances for patients who come for dialysis or radiology.

Art in Public Space

Two large works of art are situated on Wandellaan and Hospitaalpromenade. *Voortvarend* (Energetic) a large bronze by Siemen Bolhuis, was placed near the Weerwater after winning the design competition in 2009. This modern ship, 'carried by hand', is a reference to the cock-boat and Almere's past.
The copper ball by Marc Ruygrok from 1993 on Hospitaalpromenade, originally near Museum De Paviljoens, now stands on a rotating pedestal at the hospital. The word 'Hier' (Here) appears in punched-out letters.

21 Windesheim Campus

Esplanade
BDG architecten
2021-2026

The building of the Windesheim University for Applied Sciences will be providing ample meeting space, with study landscapes at the facade, green roof terraces with a view of the Weerwater lake, and a lively plinth. In the facade above the plinth to design references the parcelled polder landscape of Flevoland, which is characterised by many shades of green and a clear structure.
A block of seven storeys on the left, connected to a nine-storey block on the right via stairs, draws people into the heart of this educational building. The high glass plinths adapt in height, while the garden dances a *pas-de-deux* with the lawns on Esplanade.
A wooden construction literally forms the healthy foundation, as wood reduces stress and enhances study results. Also, wood improves humidity control. All of today's innovative knowledge is employed here to realise the study house of the future. Smart orientation towards the sun and passive solution in construction, high insulation value, and installing overhangs guarantee economic energy consumption. The atrium is designed as a large sun chimney that expels hot air by natural draught. The combination with a thermal energy system connected to the Weerwater 24 creates an integrated sustainable and healthy facility for gatherings, study, and innovation.

Studying

In Almere, studying is both small-scale and surprising, unlike in larger university towns. Almere has a number of institutes for higher education. The ROC Flevoland, Hogeschool Windesheim and two branches of Aeres: one for secondary vocational education and one University of Applied Sciences.

22 Police Station

Baljuwstraat 2
Ben Loerakker
1991-1995

The police station is a U-shaped complex with aluminium wings on a dark, receding base. On the outside, the two 'legs' of the U are mainly closed. At the entrance to the inner courtyard the corners of these legs are made of glass. The main entrance, situated on the other side of the square, has a completely glass front. The topmost of the four storeys is wider on the side of the square and is supported by slender columns. These are positioned in front of the sidewalls and are made of red cedar. The pent roof has a slightly curved profile, turning upwards a little in the direction of the inner courtyard; an architectural ordering by which the architect wishes to express the protective, safe character of this public service. By using many transparent materials at the inner courtyard, the building also speaks to the openness towards visitors and users that the police also wish to put into practice. At the back are the holding cells, parking space, and technical installations.

The 1st Big Brother House

Big Brother is watching you.
Most people will immediately think of George Orwell's *1984*, the police and the government, but in 1999 a special TV show took place in Almere: Big Brother. The Big Brother House, an idea of TV producer John de Mol, marks the beginning of reality TV. In all, 24 cameras were placed inside the house, so there was practically no room in the house that wasn't watched. In addition, there were 59 microphones to catch any and all sounds. The show had a massive following.

23 De Voetnoot (The Footnote)

Stadhuisplein 2
Tjitte Tigchelaar
1987

De Voetnoot (The Footnote) cultural centre consists of three cube-shaped parts. The lowest part is the theatre, situated in the centre, at the back. The part with an entrance on Stadhuisplein has two storeys and the one with an entrance on the other side has three. Starting at the two entrances obliquely left open in the corners at the front, passages traverse the building diagonally, ending at the theatre in the centre. On the main axis between the two higher parts is a corridor that manifests itself on the outer facade by a slight bulge. The internal structure of spaces of the same size is independent of the grey facades, which envelop it like an overcoat. This setup allows the inner space to be adapted according to need. On the inside, the various volumes were distinguished by using the colours blue and yellow. De Voetnoot is a neat example of the architecture of 1980s, when sustainability and flexibility were all the rage. Designer Tjitte Tigchelaar, who was the city architect of Almere for many years, made his most important statement for the city here.

Monument

De Voetnoot (the footnote) was added to the list of municipal monuments in 2024. Obviously because of its unique 1980s architecture, but also because this building is by now embedded in Almere's collective memory. It was the location of the first library and of the first cultural centre, the CKV. Thousands of people have literally left their traces there. Its current function as cultural breeding ground in the city centre also played a part. Music and theatre companies as well as individual artists keep this venue very much alive.

The 'Café on 2' of artist Patrick Mezas is a much-loved place for meeting other people and putting your feet up.

24 Weerwater and banks

Esplanade
Karres+Brands
2015-2025

The Weerwater ('water again') was an idea of 'godfather' Teun Koolhaas. The lake was created when sand was excavated for the A6 motorway and the railway, and it lies just north of the A6. The name is a reference to the recreated water. It is Almere's town lake, with the heart of the city on the north and the future Hortus neighbourhood on the south side. This unique area makes up the green-blue heart of Almere. It connects the city centre with the surrounding neighbourhoods, making it a crucial element in the town's identity.
Since 2015, the municipality has been developing new plans for the Weerwater and its banks, with the aim of having the city embracing the water instead of turning its back to it. To make the banks accessible in an appealing way, the Rondje Weerwater was created, a seven-kilometre route for bicycling and walking. This path, paved with blue asphalt, leads along beaches, green patches, woodlands, parks, and experimental neighbourhoods. A new bridge south of Lumièrepark divides the route into two circles of five and seven kilometres, respectively, which makes for a clever connection between the banks and Hortus. In 2025, the Weerwater will be a top location: a fine place for sports and recreation with new patches of green around the blue heart.

Alluminous

Various events take place on Esplanade throughout the year, from the Liberation Festival to the fair. In 2022, a magical light art route, known as Alluminous, was set out along the banks of the Weerwater for the first time. These special light artworks are placed on both water and land, creating an enchanting atmosphere.

25 De Fantasie (Fantasy)

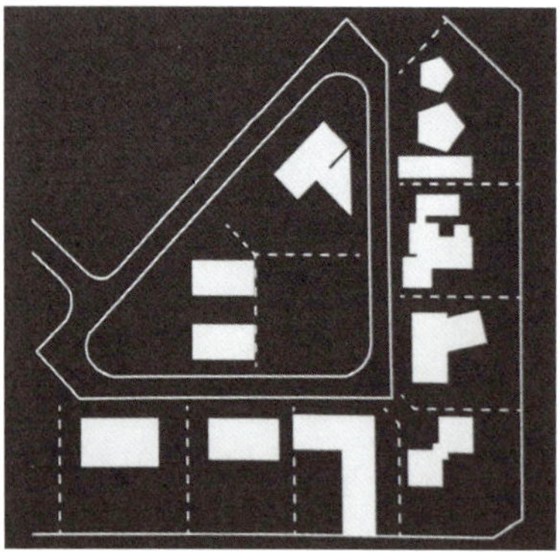

De Fantasie 1-10
Various architects
1982

Confronted with the results of the first building phase some of the more involved Almerians wondered why there was so little innovative building taking place in this new city. It turned out that the pressing load of rules and regulation simply promoted a generic building practice. In 1982, this insight led to the formation of the De Fantasie Committee and the establishment of a competition for a literally fantastic temporary dwelling under the theme 'Unusual Living'. This temporary nature meant that a lot of rules didn't apply. The RIJP was on board and made a piece of land available at the southwest point of the Weerwater lake. A veritable stream of plans was submitted, which were all assessed by the committee in terms of inventive use of material, novelty of forms of living, and originality of construction. Ten designers of houses who totally ignored all building regulations were awarded with a temporary lot of 400 m^2. These houses all stood out and the small neighbourhood soon became a magnet for visitors from the Netherlands and abroad alike. It was therefore no surprise that this temporality became permanent, and that Almere made a name for itself as the city of experimental housing architecture.

25a Hard Glas (Hard Glass)

De Fantasie 10
Benthem Crouwel
1982
Jan Benthem (exp. 1991)

The bright green dwelling Hard Glas is a house made of prefabricated board material resting on a steel load-bearing construction stabilised by Stelcon slabs. It is surrounded by willow trees. Two small stairs lead to caravan-style doors with a small window. At the front, the kitchen, bathroom, and bedroom are situated in a closed stretch of two metres wide. The living quarters beyond that feel quite spacious and are surrounded on three sides with hardened glass. An overhanging terrace adds to the spaciousness of the house. In all, an optimal result was achieved on a surface of just eight by eight metres. When a 48 m^2 annex was added to the house in 1991, it became a villa. One of the architects, Jan Benthem, lived here with his family until 2009. The house then became the home of the artist couple Fransje Killaars and Roy Villevoye.

25b House with guest room

De Fantasie 2
Jurgen van Staaden
2000-2002

This is already the second house on this location. It consists of two geometrically formed volumes in glass and aluminium, connected by a yellow footbridge. One part has two floors. The other block is very compact and serves to accommodate guests. The flower garden that enfolds it all forges the separate elements into a unity. Renate Dorrestein (1954-2018), a writer in residence in Almere in 2014, wrote her futuristic novel *Weerwater* here, which was launched in the Kunstlinie 13 in 2015.

25c Psyche and Project X

De Fantasie 8
René van Zuuk
1993; 2008

Four buckled steel H-beams form the skeleton of the house. The roof consists of two double planes, rising up like wings. The roof-gutter is situated in the middle and has a freestanding drain. The front facade looks like an eclectic collection of materials that is held in place by a broad aluminium frame. Since 2004, the architect, who designed it as a residence, continues to use it as an office space only. He moved his dwelling to Project X on the adjacent lot. The first attempt to build a house there, In Vitro, by Henk Tilder and Theo van Halewijn, was undone by force of the elements. Neighbour Van Zuuk then acquired the ruin and tore it down. The new Project X consists of a half-sunken block of anthracite concrete with a box placed perpendicularly on it, clad in grey cement-bonded fibreboards onto which a pattern of leaves was milled. The feathery Psyche and the minimalistic sculptural architecture project X go together surprisingly well.

26 Floriade Hortus District

Arboretum West a.e.
MVRDV
2022-
Winy Maas (proj.), Niek Roozen, Christian Pfeiffer (landscape)

In 2022, Almere organised the last Floriade, a world horticultural fair featuring the latest innovations in this field. The exhibition became a laboratory for studying alternative and innovative methods for greening. The Weerwatereiland, the green counterpart of the city heart, was chosen as the location. The design took into account the development of the ecological and residential Hortus neighbourhood, which would be built here after the exhibition ended. MVRDV designed the layout and the planting scheme. In the northwest were trees and bushes that started with an A, according to their Latin name; in the southeast the ones starting with a Z. Between was a tapestry of uniform lots, all with green borders of four metres wide. These lots were used for national and theme pavilions, among which purely Almerian projects such as Circuloco by Jim van der Wardt and Colours of the Sun by Bertina Slettenhaar and Mariël Bisschops stood out nicely. At the edge a number of permanent buildings arose, such as the Aeres University of Applied Sciences **27**. Utopia Eiland, on the east side of the island, is the Weerwoud foundation's prelude to the wild city park of the future.

26a Flores

Melica
Klunder Architecten
2022

Flores is a tower intended as an iconic centre of the new Hortus neighbourhood. Flores is located exactly in the middle of the former Floriade grounds and its glass facade cladding absorbs the colours of all the plant species from the tree collection planted there by MVRDV. The artist Alex Verhaest and social design studio Arttenders matched images from books of plant albums until these fused into a single image. The title of the work is *Sympoiesis*, which means co-creation. The result is a sea of glowing colours on a 100 × 42 metre surface. Starting somewhat dark at the foot of the building, then fiery, and further upwards picking up more blue from the sky. It is a tower that radiates its glorious colours for miles around.

26b M.

Melica 200
Studio Ossidiana
2022

The home base of M., which is the prelude to an Almerian art museum, consists of three circular parts that appear to be floating in the water: a ring-shaped access road, a patio within it, and an exhibition space. Pink is the principal colour. The inner wall of the drum-shaped museum hall is made of polycarbonate. Inside, geometrical shapes, functioning as windows, light up behind a transparent curtain. The reception desk is made of pink terrazzo into which locally found shells have been incorporated. This material was also used in the ring road in front of the 'drum', augmented with diamond-shaped intarsia. The idea is for the water square to be used as a second exhibition space and the round patio as a stage. M. was nominated for the Mies van der Rohe Award 2024.

27 Aeres University of Applied Sciences

Arboretum West 98
BDG architecten
2022-2024
Wilco Scheffer (proj.)

Together with the Innovation Pavilion of the province of Flevoland, the Aeres University of Applied Sciences makes up the Flevo Campus, an education and research square in the field of innovation in food production and urban greening. The building suits this purpose. It is set up as a series of flexible spaces for working, learning, and researching in many different ways. From the main hall, which also houses the canteen, broad stairs of recycled wood lead upwards. On the roof, leisure space was created with benches and duckboards made of wood from old canal barges.

The benches meander among an enormous variety of plants and trees. Above them hangs a screen of tilted panels that both filter the sunlight and generate energy. Two of the facades have hanging gardens around the window sections. These plants help cool the interior spaces and are mostly sprinkled with rainwater from the roof. The walls are made of bio-composites here. Another facade is covered with a curtain of solar panels. The floors and ceilings are made of recycled materials and the furniture consists of refurbished pieces that now look new and crisp. This building, called de Groene Long (the Green Lung), is a zero-energy and circular building. With its innovative technology it takes a significant step towards realising healthy, sustainable architecture.
Winner Circular Award 2022

The Oldest Tree

In the Weerwater lies Weerwatereiland, which was included in the design for the Floriade in its entirety. Many years ago, a group of people, including councillor Adri Duivesteijn, visited the island on a boat excursion. They were looking for trees that would fit in the Floriade Park under construction, including the so-called 'oldest tree', pointed out by Duivesteijn. The route of the A6 motorway, originally planned here, was still clearly visible. Eventually, the road followed a more southern course. One of the participants found the tiny skull of a small fox here.

28 Beatrixpark

Beatrixpromenade
Bureau Bakker en Bleeker
1981

Almere derives its special character from how city and nature are intertwined. Each district is surrounded by green, and green wedges penetrate deep into the residential areas. The extensive Beatrixpark is one of the pillars of the inner-city greenery and is regarded as Almere's Central Park. B+B, a firm that advocates the application of landscape architecture to cities, first designed just a framework for this large area of 125 hectares (310 acres). The backbone is a straight canal that connects to the Noorderplassen and the Weerwater lake. It is a rectilinear design with massive wooded areas and broad footpaths. Long sightlines and spaciousness predominate.
In 1997 the parks initial setup was ready to be refined. In the makeover, the same designers introduced a more intensive part with new facilities such as a circuit for inline skating and sports fields, as well as an extensive part of a more secluded nature.
The park was named after Queen Beatrix when she planted a lime tree on the occasion of the fifth anniversary of the city. Along the straight footpath an authentic American diner from 1939 joins a prefabricated wooden pavilion.

Nimis

On an island in the canal, artist Pjotr Müller built the small Nimis temple in 1989. It adorns the park like a modern folly. For the entrance at Muziekdreef he designed a two-part stainless-steel cage with a zigzag roof, complete with polyester birds. In 2021, Almerian artists paid homage to these works with interventions that stimulate the senses during the Nachtvisie (night vision) project. The more artists and urban dwellers add in the form of activities, the more meaningful the park becomes to the city.

29 Stedenwijk Noord district/ Petting Zoo

Heerenveenpad; Heerenveenpad 43
19 het atelier; 70F Architecture
2008-2012; 2008
Rob Moritz (proj.); Bas ten Brinke (proj.)

Stedenwijk Noord, completed in 1979, was in urgent need of a facelift by 2008. Subsidence, overdue maintenance, and low building quality had caused the neighbourhood to deteriorate both socially and aesthetically. The renovation, in Amsterdam School style, brought relief to the residents. The old grey bricks were replaced with slender red ones with recessed joints and the cavity walls were widened for better insulation. Window frames became more varied and double glazing was fitted. Through refinement and variation in brickwork and roof tiles the neighbourhood acquired more status, identity, and landmarks, without losing its original character. Sandstone reliefs by Annet van der Kamp depict the characteristics of the provinces after which the housing blocks were named. Greenery maintenance was also improved. In the nearby Den Uylpark a petting zoo was realised, designed by Bas ten Brinke of 70F Architecture. This sober but perfectly executed building made of wood and acrylate board is a showpiece of the neighbourhood. In the morning the shutters open and in the evening, they close, automatically. The rigid outer form and consistent austerity in the use of materials make it a valuable asset for the neighbourhood.

Nature Studio

In the Den Uylpark we find the dye plant field. The field is open to the public and information signs have been placed near the plants. Here, the IVN (an institute for nature education) together with the members of the Wolunie (wool union) grows the plans that are used to dye wool. This wool comes from the Almerian sheep herd. Until recently, the fleece were thought of as worthless, but now they have found a new application. Using innovative techniques, the wool can be used as insulation material. Textile artist Bertina Slettenhaar creates woollen and felt designs that she dyes with the plants from this field.

30 Casa Casla

Weerwaterplein 3
Lanoire & Courrian
2006-2007
Jean Philippe Lanoire,
Sophie Courrian (proj.)

Casa Casla is architecturally geared to its original function as a centre for architecture, with an open office floor at the top, two storage rooms, leisure and meeting spaces, and a large, sloping exhibition room. The transparent plinth with public spaces bears a protruding volume with a glass facade at the front. One can 'climb' the building from the street, as the roof is constructed as a stairway leading to an observation point on the protruding part of the building. Everything, including the stairs and the space around the building is paved with special, oblong, dark-brown clinkers, making for an optimal embedding in the public space. When the architectural centre had to go, a number of alternative functions were tested. Since 2023, the building has been in use as an office and debating centre.

Gone Forever

CASLA stands for Centre for Architecture, Urbanity, and Landscape of Almere. The organisation moved into the building in 2006, providing important information about the development of the young city. Its initiatives included Young Monuments Day, Architecture Day, and the Almere Architecture Award, as well as exhibitions about individual architects, comparisons with similar cities, views on City and Nature and on urban developments. CASLA also organised tours of the city and national and international excursions. They provided information

and publications on Almere's DNA, a role that was lost when the organisation was discontinued.

Infrastructure

The extensive network of paved bicycle paths in Almere is quite something. It stretches over 500 kilometres, of which 440 kilometres are exclusively for bicycles. Wherever these paths cross other roads, bicycles have right of way. At main roads the crossings are on separate levels, via hundreds of bridges and tunnels. Now that the greenery has matured, riding a bicycle in the city landscape is a real pleasure. In addition, the bus lanes also have their own separate circuit, like an aboveground metro network, but more practical, as ambulances and police vehicles can also use it.

When Almere was conceived, in the 1970s, there was much turmoil about oil. In order to save fuel, there were Car-Free Sundays. In 1972, the Club of Rome published the report *Limits to Growth*, a serious encouragement to reduce the use of cars and promote public transport. Almere's planners found inspiration in the new town of Runcorn near Liverpool, where the first rapid bus transport system of the world was created in 1971. The motorway network there, which is exclusively used by buses, is completely separated from all other traffic. Almere has Runcorn to thank for its beautiful bicycle paths and its system of separate bus lanes and it was believed that this setup would automatically reduce automobile traffic. The vast majority of residences were to be within a 15-minute walk from a bus stop. This principle was maintained in most places, although, for financial reasons, the frequency of the buses had to be lowered, a number of bus stops were cancelled, and Oosterwold is still rather isolated in terms of public transport. Along all bus lanes fences protect pedestrians from whizzing busses. At crossings with other transport systems there are traffic lights that always turn to green for approaching buses. By now, 166 cities have adopted similar systems.

Almere is quite sprawled. Its six train stations provide access to everywhere. Motor traffic is served by the A6 motorway, with the districts Haven and Hout to the south, and curves slightly near Stad. Initially, a very straight route had been planned, but this plan had to be adapted when the Weerwater lake 24 was created in 1988. Broad lanes run between the districts, surrounded by noise barriers that hide the built-up area from view in most cases. Residential neighbourhoods here are predominantly low-traffic. Many people are surprised by the number of bumps, which aim to reduce speed. Those who choose to use a car will simply have to deal with these bumps, and likewise with the fact that the route from A to B is always much longer for cars than for buses or bicycles.

31 BouwRAI 1 Muziekwijk
31a Studio Houses

Wessel Ilckenstraat 2-32
Herman Hertzberger
1988-1990

31b Multi-phase Dwellings

Wessel Ilckenstraat
Teun Koolhaas
1988-1990

In April 1990, the BouwRAI of the National Building Council was organised for the fifth time in Amsterdam. A completely new element of this trade fair for building and living was an outdoor 'life-size' exhibition in Almere. The municipality of Almere saw an opportunity to lure potential residents and build a young and innovative image. This first edition was held in Muziekwijk Oost. Under the banner of 'pioneering building' projects were started by corporations, developers, and pension funds. Clients and architects could experiment to their heart's content and the results didn't disappoint. Important steps were taken in finding new combinations of living and working for the old and the young, for families and individuals.
Sixteen dwellings 31a in groups of four, each based on a floor plan of eight-by-eight metres, one corner of which is cut off to serve as an outdoor space. The living room, which borders the cut-off corner, has a glass facade and a view of the inner garden. All houses have a room on the roof that is accessed via a spiral staircase on the outer wall, which creates the option of establishing a work spot with its own entrance.
A terraced house 31b that can be split into two parts, making it suitable for simultaneous occupation by seniors and young families. The ground and first floor have separate entrances in the sturdy entrance hall that is rounded-off at the back and was placed in front of the flat facade. The facade and entrance are finished with aluminium profile plates, which gives these dwellings a businesslike, industrial look.

31c Women-friendly Living

Glenn Millerweg
Luzia Hartsuyker-Curjel
1988-1990

In the 1980s, Luzia Hartsuyker-Curjel began to design alternative, women-friendly dwellings in response to traditional living structures. She had an eye for alternative ways of living together, with floor plans that expressed equality. This shows in equal-sized rooms that all have equal access to the kitchen and bathroom. For the 1990 outdoor exhibition she designed ten state-subsidised private houses in two storeys. Hartsuyker-Curjel combined a mezzanine at the back with high windows at the front to let daylight penetrate the entire house: the suncatcher. With her eye for detail, she disguised a radiator as a railing for the mezzanine.

32 De Toonladder (The Scale)

Kathleen Ferrierstraat 51
Kuiper Compagnons
1990-1993
Wytze Patijn, Koos Kok (proj.)

De Toonladder introduces a new living concept for seniors. It combines facilities for various gradations of care, so that people can move house internally when their need of care increases. The project stands out in the neighbourhood with a palette of light, cheerful colours, with mainly much yellow and blue and a bright red door here and there. On the west side, the building makes an elegant curve. The independent apartments there have a front door on the outside of the curve, with the care facilities situated on the inside. The adjacent complex features care apartments along galleries. At the centre of the spacious inner garden is the octagonal 'Concertmaster', where residents can play cards, do their laundry, or relax on the terrace. On the east side of the access road that connects the complex with the neighbourhood is a row of low villas with red pyramid roofs in leafy surroundings. These 'Quartets' each provide space for four independent living units. Two of these, the 'Menuets', are reserved for Alzheimer's patients. In the middle of the complex are a petting zoo and a unit for people with acquired brain injuries. The entire ensemble is a showcase of beautiful and varied care architecture that is superbly embedded in the neighbourhood.

In Violation of Regulation!

Jan de Vetter, director of housing corporation Groene Stad Almere, applied for a subsidy for this complex with both the Ministry of Housing and that of Public Health. Two types of funding that had been completely separated up till then. Then State Secretary Enneüs Heerma was impressed with the initiative when visiting the project during construction: 'If my mother would still be alive, I would sign her up for this, Jan, but it violates all regulation!'
Heerma then 'stalled' his decision on the official negative advice about the subsidy application to his department for so long, that rejecting it was no longer an option. And so this extraordinary combination of fine social housing near good care facilities became a reality.

33 De Muzen (The Muses)

Louis Davidsstraat
Atelier Pro
1993-1997
Leon Thier, Noud te Riele,
Arjan Oosterhof (proj.)

This residential building for seniors at the head of the Muzenpark is 360 metres long and has a Mediterranean ambience. The apricot colour of the walls is inspired by the French city of Toulouse. The elongated, slightly curved facade has staggered balconies on the park side that are connected by slender steel poles. Bicyclists can directly access the Muzenpark via two high underpasses. The wings are three storeys high, and the middle section has five storeys. Here, the upper storey lies far back under a light-tinted overhang. This storey is finished in dark-stained wood, giving the building a finishing frame that unifies the building volume. At the other side, on Louis Davidssstraat, four blocks with a tulip-like floor plan connect with the facade. These are intended for communal facilities and for overnight guests of the occupants of the 167 units. Between the main building and these blocks, we find the glass-roofed atrium, galleries, transparent lift shafts, and stairwells. The beautiful greenery by Bureau Copijn not only provides a pleasantly calm environment but also inspires people to meet and become active. All the apartments and maisonettes have a living room facing the park.

Without a Trace

At the back of De Muzen lies Muzenpark, with a trail that leads along 53 types of trees. There is a pond where there used to be a wooden wind vane with four human figures, made by the artist Stephan Balkenhol. Nobody knows how this vane disappeared. Even the model, property of housing corporation De Alliantie who commissioned it, is gone without a trace. The Muzenpark also has the Singing Bicycle Path, where everyone is officially allowed to sing (along) while cycling, without feeling embarrassed.

34 Groeiwoningen (Growth Houses)

Jan Hanlostraat
Atelier Herman Hertzberger (AHH)
1998-2002

The idea behind these houses is simple. A series of basic dwellings consists of a long rectangular volume of two storeys that are linked to the next house in the row via a smaller rectangular volume of one storey. This creates a row of serially linked houses with HH shapes. In these in-between spaces individual wishes for growth can be realised. In some cases, additional living space was built in this zone, sometimes also with an extra bedroom on the first floor. At other houses residents opted for a kind of sun lounge with a glass covering, for all sorts of activities. Another variant is a tower-like structure with a garage and extra bedrooms. Most of the owners opted for a glass linking structure that they use in various ways. And sometimes the space was left open, so residents can decide what to do with it at a later date. The consistent dimensioning allows for these extensions. The different choices of individual occupants resulted in a varying architectural image within a clear frame. The end facades are made of grey bricks and the side walls are clad in horizontal hardwood boards.

Growing!

Almere is the fastest growing city in the Netherlands, with an expected future population of 350,000.
Here, in 1995, artist Marte Röling, Royal Commissioner Han Lammers and mayor Ralph Pans are awaiting the planting of the first of the 100 trees that symbolise the 100,000 residents of Almere.

35 Maliebaan

Arthur van Schendelpad
Kuiper Compagnons
1998-2003
Wytze Patijn (proj.)

A school with a playground, 80 patio houses, and 126 rented houses around a large interior space. The two parts with apartments on the side of the street differ in height and are linked via a glass overhead bridge above a bicycle and foot path. At the interior side the broadly cantilevered roof edge of the higher parts of the building is supported by slender, slightly angled steel columns, a hallmark of the architecture of Wytze Patijn.

The patio houses are placed in a spacious square around a car-free inner space. The raised white 'steps' that are placed against the facades in lieu of small front gardens are eagerly made use of by the residents, who adorn them with trinkets and plants. The stairwells are situated in round, tower-like structures. A high, covered, and enclosed garden with luxurious green underlines the coherence between inside and outside as a quality of living in this complex.

Sliding

In 2020, the Odyssee school by architectural firm GAJ/VBW was completed in the Homerus neighbourhood. Whereas the school at Maliebaan is completely integrated in the building block, this building prominently stands in the neighbourhood as an independent entity. The bright green and yellow colours on the outside are repeated in the interior, where they are complemented by red and blue furniture. There is a playground on the roof, with a very nice feature: when the students want to go down again, they can choose between stairs or a slide!

36 Sint Bonifatius Church

Contrabasweg 239
Royal HaskoningDHV
2019-2022
Jurgen Boonstra (proj.)

The exterior presents two building volumes: the space on the ground floor made of sand-coloured facades with on both sides two wooden, half-round recesses and a wooden daylight construction on the roof. A classical scheme was applied: a nave and two side aisles, with an apse at the end. In the back is a reception space. The interior is subdued, based on the architectural influences of Dom Hans van der Laan of the Bossche School. The skylight provides natural light, running all along the length of the nave. In dimensioning and use of colour the architect had to take into account a particular demand: placing a 27-metre-long artwork by the French-Russian painter Théodore Strawinsky. This work became the starting point for the design and is now the *pièce de résistance* of the church.
It depicts the life of Christ in 25 paintings in soft pastel tints that are also used in the interior. The artwork was saved from the Willebrordkerk in Almelo, which was demolished in 2005. The 'Strappo method' was used: the stucco was transferred to cheesecloth by using Italian animal glue. The cloth was then transferred to a latex underlayer and mounted on canvas stretchers.

Religion

Jurgen Boonstra: 'Nowhere in our country more new catholic churches are being built than here. In contrast to the national trend, the number of Roman Catholics has been growing in Almere these past few years.'
The foundation for the St. Bonifatius church was laid in 2019.
Worshippers find the church light and airy. Daylight from the skylights falls on panels painted by Théodore Stravinsky, grandson of Igor Stravinsky. Here they shine again.

Bridges

Almere, 'reclaimed from the Zuiderzee', is around five metres below sea level, which makes good water management of vital importance. The Hoge and Lage Vaart are crucial drainage elements, in combination with an intricate system of lakes, waterways and ditches. Crossing these waterways requires many bridges. Almere has 737 of them, which is more than Venice, which has 400 bridges.

The Stichtse Brug and Hollandse Brug are the main traffic bridges providing access to the city. In addition, there are hundreds of foot and bicycle bridges of which around one hundred are made of wood, built over the past 35 years. There are a few interesting ones designed by architects.

Almerian architect René van Zuuk designed a number of special bridges for the city. His bicycle/pedestrian bridge across the Olstgracht is 42 metres long and 9 metres wide, connecting Stedenwijk and Stadshart. This steel cable bridge with slanted pylons from 2004 is a reference to sailboat masts. The Limburgse Brug from 2021 is a small concrete bridge with a striking Corten steel parapet. It replaces an old wooden bicycle bridge that was at the end of its life span. The punched-out motif in the bridge, a design by Willem van der Laan, is the logo of Rondje Weerwater 24. The bridge is part of the bicycle route around the city lake, transforming it from an uneventful place into a connecting element between adjacent neighbourhoods.

Gert-Jan de Jong designed the Tweede Levenbrug, a pedestrian bridge to the Floriade 26. He reused existing infrastructure materials such as old supporting beams, and benches. The straight bridge of over 130 metres long connects various parts of Hortus.

In 2022, the Weerwaterbrug by Quist Wintermans Architects was opened. This design won the competition for a solution to divide the Weerwater 24 – with a diameter of seven kilometres – into two parts. The 234-metre-long bridge starts at the little beach in Lumièrepark, making an elegant line to the Floriade grounds. To stay in tune with the theme of 'Growing Green Cities', various sustainable elements that fit the theme were applied in the bridge. The choice for concrete may seem to contradict this, but by pouring the columns and the road surface in one go without any seams, a longer life span is aimed for. Applying waterproof concrete also contributes to this. People, plants, and animals were taken into account. Pleasant seats at the bends in the bridge provide enjoyable views and along the banks, holes for nesting and hotels for insects were realised. By placing only two streetlights on the bridge, light pollution is prevented. These lights are powered by solar panels on the bridge and they only go on when human activity is detected.

Boelijn drawbridge

Between Kettingsteek and Jakobsstaf, in the Noorderplassen neighbourhood, lies the elegant Boelijn drawbridge (2005), designed by Lukassen Brokking. This bright white, open steel construction leans backwards and has two protruding elements that can lift up the bridge using steel cables. The bridge makes one immediately think of legs and arms and with its charming silhouette it is truly an asset for this neighbourhood.

The rounded-off, fixed part of the bridge folds like a ladder with openings in its sides across the road, providing enough counterweight to lift up the counterpart nestled within the curve.

Land Art

In landscape art, or Land Art, artists use elements of the landscape in which they are realising their work. This may be the soil, or the air, but also the history or character of the spot. In order to understand these works one has to look at what a work specifically does to the environment it is in. Does it tell or change something about that spot? Does it comment upon the environment or the condition of the earth or does it direct one's attention to certain facts or characteristics? Land Art started in the US in the 1970s, when the first images of our planet seen from space became available and many values were up for debate. People realised that art had fallen victim to commercialism. Museums had become institutes with much power over art and the artists. By making nature their working ground artists attempted to evade that power. One artist drove a bronze rod one kilometre into the ground. Another one had a huge piece of a mountain removed and called the space where nothing was left a 'negative sculpture'. These were often quite big interventions that involved a lot of money all the same and that were eventually usurped anyway because they required maintenance and the artists made money from selling aerial photos and footage. By coincidence, a collection of land art pieces accumulated in the province of Flevoland. Only here there was enough room for a replica of *Observatory* by Robert Morris, a work that was supposed to disappear after the exhibition 'Sonsbeek Buiten de Perken' (Sonsbeek beyond the boundaries) in Arnhem ended, in 1971, but got a second lease on life this way. It turned out to be the start of the Flevoland collection of by now ten works, two of which are in Almere.

Groene Kathedraal (Green Cathedral)

First, the floor plan of the thirteenth-century cathedral of Reims (FR) was laid out in the ground of the polder in white bands of concrete. In the spots where in Reims the columns and buttresses stood, artist Marinus Boezem placed beds of shells and planted 187 Italian poplars there that shot up like spears. On an aerial photograph, it is as if one looks down along the pillars towards the ribs of the distant canopy of heaven. When walking between the rustling trees, one sees the treetops caressing the air.

Marinus Boezem felt that the brave citizens of Almere who started their new lives on the ground were in need of such a 'building'. Nearby he carved out the form of the church in the forest. By the time the poplars of the cathedral will die of old age and the concrete bands become overgrown, the shape will still remain in the forest as a memory of what nature reclaimed.

Top: Groene Kathedraal (Green Cathedral), Marinus Boezem, 1996; 2022
Bottom: Pampushavenweg, Daniel Libeskind, 1997

Polderland Garden of Love and Fire

Besides the strip with upright aluminium boards in the dark gravel that reflect the sunlight in fine weather, this artwork includes two wide ditches and a footpath. They make lines in the landscape that, when followed through, point to Paris, Salamanca, and Berlin. Salamanca, the city of San Juan de la Cruz, the mystic whose poem 'O Living Flame of Love' inspired Libeskind to make this work of art; Paris, the city of poet Paul Celan; and Berlin, the city where Libeskind was living at the time. He wanted to make a place for meditation, but true to its name it developed into a well-known cruising area. The work is an easy prey for vandalism and is not always in perfect condition.

37 Noorderplassen

Hoge Ring a.e.
Jan Wouter Bruggenkamp,
Reinier Nijland
1976-1990

By deciding to also start extracting sand for housing and infrastructural projects within the city limits, landscape designer Jan Wouter Bruggenkamp took the first step in creating the Noorderplasssen. His idea was for the area to become an appealing buffer zone between the city and the Lepelaarsplassen with their wet grasslands around it. This was realised by situating housing and bars and restaurants there. This was done on a number of piers on the south side. Here we also find De Realiteit 39 and the last remaining farm barn. A strip of woodland and beaches, connected to Beatrixpark via the Noorderleepad and Clauspad, is the finishing touch.
On the northeast side are a number of islands bearing names such as Muiterseiland (Mutineers Island), Pirateneiland (Pirates Island), Zeeroverseiland (Buccaneers Island), and Schateiland (Treasure Island), where campsite Waterhout is situated. This is also the start of the Lepelaarpad, which runs all the way to Oostvaardersdijk and the houses of Noorderplassen West. This is a neighbourhood with many water dwellings, the urban development plan of which was made by Bureau KCAP. The buildings here are surrounded by green and water on all sides.
Long before the principle of 'Connect City and Nature' was included in the Almere Principles in 2008, Noorderplassen really lived up to it.

37a Casa Mirador

Stopperknoop 46
Arc2 architectuur
2011-2013
Gert-Jan de Jong, Eric Goldhoorn (proj.)

A villa with a roof terrace, and a living room on the second floor. That was what the occupants wanted, so that they would have a grand view of the Markermeer lake from their living room. The room features a bay window in the shape of a cut crystal protruding from the building. The pointed shape and oblique lining of the bay window are repeated in the facade cladding. This consists partly of wood, painted orange. The plinth is made of wire-cut bricks with reliefs in shades of brown and orange that connect the building to the ground.

37b Ripken House

Stopperknoop 2
Lars Courage
2011

Courage favours techniques from commercial and industrial construction and likes the colour black. With this house of steel, he won the Almere architecture award 2012. The double front door is almost obscured in the closed facade of profiled sheet. Above it is a facade-wide panoramic window providing light far into the open living quarters.

37c Golden Mile

Grootzeil, Spiegel, Gangboord
Theo Verburg
2004-2007

This complex has 54 upstairs and downstairs apartments, with high windows on the four sides facing the streets. The anthracite brick forms a pleasant contrast with the orange roof with its shifting ridge. The roof protrudes far over the terrace duckboards at the front doors and is supported by thin steel columns. The facades buckle outwards and inwards and have large openings and entrances to the inner courtyard. The street sites are pleasantly expressive. The inner courtyard with its fences, sheds, and parking spaces is cluttered.

38a Eenvoud (Simplicity)

De Eenvoud 1-15
Various architects
2007-2013

Eenvoud (Simplicity) is the result of the third competition organised by De Fantasie Committee, in 2006. The assignment was to design a very sober, detached house. The designation 'temporary' no longer applied, even though the aim still was to avoid limitations that might arise from regulations.

The Building Inspection agreed to respect the choice of the jury and to interpret the regulations generously. Nevertheless, some difficulties arose during the realisation phase. The building location was changed. The building lots had to be purchased by the winners and if construction didn't start at the appointed date, there were fines to be paid. Some of the winners were forced to look for others to take over the plan.

Top: Mirror House, De Eenvoud, Anouk Vogel, Johan Selbing, 2013
Bottom: De Korf (The Hive), De Eenvoud, MADEarchitecten, Klaas Kloosterboer, 2012

38b Clearing

De Eenvoud
Frank Görge, Carola Görge
2013

Those who visit Eenvoud today, will mainly see large houses on compact lots. Clearing and De Korf (The Hive) on numbers 5 and 6 fit the original assignment best because of their size, inventive use of materials, and distinguishing shape. Rubberhuis stands out with its contrast between the wood of the basic structure and the black EPDM roofing, which runs partly over the walls. Spiegelhuis (mirror house), a rectangle that appears to be floating above a narrow, recessed plinth, was initially called Cache-Cache, as the house would be hiding itself in the mirrored surroundings. There is one large interior space. Functional elements are placed alongside the outer walls, forming one continuous piece of furniture.

38c Type EW-58/08

De Eenvoud
Matton Office
2018
Ton Matton (proj.)

The house of straw finished with clay (Type EW-58/08) is based on the standardised post-war housing types that were developed in the former GDR by architect Wilfried Stallknecht. People could construct them themselves using prefab building materials. Differences came about because everyone would fit the parts together in a slightly different way. Initially, Ton Matton had the idea to demolish such a house in East Germany and rebuild it in the Netherlands, but this proved too cumbersome. So, new construction it was. The buyer of the plan was given an extensive manual for building the house, starting with a site hut, compost toilet, rain barrel, and wheelbarrow. The result was a friendly house with a red tiled roof surrounded by a garden full of flowers and fruit. In addition to the manual, Matton gave the proprietress much advice about sober and autarchic living, which she took very much to heart.

39 De Realiteit (Reality)

De Realiteit 7-27
Various architects
1987

Elaborating on the idea of De Fantasie 25 the Fantasie Committee organised a second competition in 1985. This time the theme was simply 'Temporary Living'. In assessing the 182 entries the focus was on sustainability and originality. Like before, the 17 winners were each given a lot of 400 m^2 near the Noorderplassen, but, as with De Fantasie, they couldn't go to commercial banks to finance construction because there would be no solid collateral. The winning designs were all self-built and self-financed, with additional sponsoring by suppliers in the form of building materials.

Now, 25 years on, maintenance of many of the objects is somewhat overdue. Strictly speaking, permanent occupancy is only allowed here when the ground on which the houses stand is also the property of the owners, which is a recipe for degradation.
In all, the project is a good example of the enormous creativity that is unleashed when the right stimulus is provided. The variety in solutions that are grouped together here tells a tale about the state of affairs in building technique and material development in the 1980s, and of how sustainability was viewed at the time. De Realiteit is a manifesto of the unparalleled design inventiveness that this competition tapped into.

39a Markies/OPENHuis

De Realiteit 25
Eduard Böhtlingk
1986; 1995

A caravan named Markies that becomes three times as big when the sides with the striped awnings are opened. It is parked in a corner of the garden, while the owner was building his OPENhuis: a mobile unit of 3 by 10 metres, standing at the front of the lot against the fence. An overgrown pergola above it provides protection from the hot sun. OPENhuis can be almost fully opened on the side of the garden. All the facilities are cleverly placed against the back wall. Markies has travelled all over the world and has inspired designers to come up with similar solutions.

39b Polderblik (Polder View)

De Realiteit 7
Teun Koolhaas
1987

Polderblik is a house made of aluminium, steel, anchor cables, glass, and wood, with a spectacular view of the polder. The construction consists of seven bays, three of which have floor-to-ceiling windows with a remarkable glazing bar arrangement. This is where the entrance is, which was conceived as a greenhouse and heat buffer. The living quarters are on the first floor, which has a balcony that extends far under the slightly curved roof of corrugated aluminium, which is 'detached' from the house by horizontal window strips.

39c Boven de Zeespiegel (Above Sea Level)

De Realiteit 13
Jan Wagenaar, Hans Weijsenfeld
1987

A house consisting of two units, painted yellow, with a long stairway in the middle. It stands on high poles, as the designers figured that they had to take into account the tides and the rising sea level. The glass facades come from greenhouses.

39d Diogenes II

De Realiteit 19
Maarten Meijs
1987

Convenient, such a featherlight house that can be taken apart and rebuilt elsewhere. Even the foundation and piping can be disassembled. The house has much glass on both the front and back with large French windows opening to a terrace and garden. Sanitary facilities, cupboards and kitchen elements are located against the outer walls. The large open space can be used in many ways. It is an example of how De Realiteit was decades ahead of the current penchant for tiny houses.

40 BouwRAI 2 Filmwijk

Filmwijk Noord Almere Stad
Gemeente Almere
1992

This second outdoor exposition of the BouwRAI was a great boost for the special, innovative building style that would become Almere's hallmark. The theme of 'pioneering building' radically transcended the ingrained traditions and rules with regard to building houses and facilities that had such a firm grip on the world of construction at the time. In the Filmwijk neighbourhood, future living was to become tangible. There was a demand for visionary designs, for proposals that broke with convention and demonstrated a range of remarkable interiors and exteriors. It was all about experimenting and responding to the changing nature of households and living together; and to all those people that make up the Dutch population who have different wishes, cultures, and customs. And it worked. Filmwijk is still popular as an outdoor exhibition of how things can be done fundamentally different. To give designers maximum freedom, an urban plan was made only later, based on the designs. The core of the plan was an avenue of trees in the shape of a semicircle, Hollywoodlaan. From the centre of the imaginary full circle streets radiate towards the avenue like the spokes of a wheel. All of the submitted designs were accepted and there was room for all of them. In all, 588 houses were built by thirty combinations of architect and client.

40a Health Centre

Greta Garboplantsoen 1
Aldo van Eyck, Julyan Wickham
1989-1992

The health centre is a low, triangular building with rounded corners, with one side aligned straight along the bus lane. On that side the architect placed a series of streetlamps that look like embattlements, with square windows under all of them. The two other sides have a more open structure with large windows. The entrances are situated on the notched-in shortest side, exactly where the facades bent invitingly inwards. The interior space is structured by a long, straight street with consultation rooms and surgeries on one side and multifunctional spaces with playfully curved walls on the other. The interior is very colourful. The outer walls are covered in purple plaster.

40b Polygoon School

Hollywoodlaan 109
Herman Hertzberger
1992-1995

Sixteen low, sunny classrooms are situated along a high corridor under a curved roof of profile sheet that spreads its wings protectively to just over the classrooms. This corridor is actually the core of the building. All the classrooms open up to it and it is filled with things that inspire students to learn. It's where they meet each other and exchanges take place. With this building the architect expressly stimulates encounters, the central theme in his work. Perpendicular to this volume is the white main building with the offices and the high gym.

40c Modern Acropolism

James Stewartstraat
Soeters van Eldonk
1992

With its colourful wooden facades under a curved roof profile, this row of houses stands out among the many special housing projects of Filmwijk. The semi-detached houses are placed on a continuous red plinth that houses functional spaces such as kitchens and storage. The living room and terrace are on the first floor. Above that is space for bedrooms. The plinth is hidden in the greenery, making it look as if the houses are built on a hill. A modern Acropolis.

41 Polderburen

Schietwilgsingel 2
Hans Ruijssenaars
1994-1995

Three sides of this residential care facility complex have independent living units that are accessed from the surrounding streets. At their backs are a series of single and twin-bedded rooms with sanitary facilities. Between these rooms and the spacious inner garden is a covered interior street, via which everyone can reach the main building located on the fourth side. The facade is partly finished in wooden strips that are painted bright yellow. At the entrance door the walls curve elegantly inwards. In front is a row of slender, grey steel columns on slightly thicker, round bases. These support wooden steplike notched-in beams under a protruding roof. Across from the main entrance are the doors to the inner garden. There too are steel columns in front of the facades. Their green hue is repeated in the doors of the four pavilions that are scattered in the garden. There is a restaurant there and all kinds of activities are organised in them. Two of the pavilions are round, spreading their ceiling beams like the ribs of an umbrella. In the centre are four columns under a glass lantern. Between the beams running to this central point a circle of grooves was made of yellow glass, illuminating the spaces underneath with a warm light.

Paradise

Architect Hans Ruijssenaars primary goal was to provide residents with a sense of home.
'Especially in places where care increases, living tends to become less important. But also when they need full care, people are still living there and the home and institute can contribute to that universal feeling of "home",' Ruijssenaars wrote on his website. He reached his goal. The architecture of Polderburen is all about warmth and that sense of belonging. One resident, who called himself Adam, was sitting on

the padded couch underneath the yellow light slits and said that he was in Paradise.

42 Dôme and Cube

Veluwezoom 5-7
KOW Architecten
2002; 2007
Frans Dirks, Hans Kuiper

This steel 'spaceship', which is connected to a cube-shaped volume, is situated in a prominent spot at the junction of Veluwedreef and the A6 motorway. With its location on the motorway and spectacular form the complex functions as an icon and identifier of Almere.
The main shape of the Dôme is a flattened sphere on a cylindrical pedestal, reminiscent of a UFO. The windows of the three storeys in the sphere are lined up neatly. In front of the four steel-skinned storeys of the Cube coloured screens have been placed. Both units feature an atrium with a glass roof and circular galleries. They are connected via a footbridge and a cone-shaped entrance section. The rippling waters of the moat at the front brings the facades to life.
The complex was built as a fashion centre. Big brands rented units here and held fashion shows, after which the clothes found their way to the fashion stores. Initially, the plan was to add a triangular and fan-shaped unit, but this proved to be too ambitious. Since 2022, Cube and Dôme are used as a multifunctional business centre and event space, while waiting for new tenants.

Ruins

This replica under construction of a castle in the Belgian town of Jemeppe became decrepit pretty soon after building began in 2000. It was intended as a convention centre with a luxury hotel, a coach house, stables, ponds, and a vast herb garden where Almerians could stroll freely.
The financing, however, was not sound and the bank halted construction. The elements then had free reign of the open structure. Although new initiatives were started to rescue the project, these all failed. And thus, the young city involuntarily gained an unwished-for romantic touch. For many years now, the castle has been home to owls.

43 Doemere

New Yorkweg
Bakker & Verhoeff
1985-1988

The municipal designers of Almere Buiten had the idea that larger homeware shops – which are usually located at the edges of cities – deserved a more central place in this part of the city. In 1985 a competition was held for a concentration of megastores around a large parking lot next to the existing shopping centre at Buiten Station. The winning design by Chiel Verhoeff features a dozen simple halls that are connected by striking tent constructions above the entrances. These consist of white pointed caps of steel and cloth that stick out above everything else. The architecture brings up associations with fairgrounds and festivals and immediately lends a festive air to shopping.
From the very start, Doemere was an innovative concept with much appeal. The focus is on spending leisure time, which is also evident from the materials used.
The 53-metre steel tower with a light globe in top, marks a bold choice. For Almerians, Doemere has become a landmark.

Irreparable

De Beurs by architectural firm Environmental Design was one of the first business centres in Almere. It was built in 1982 and demolished in 2021, removing the only building in Almere that was related to brutalism: an unadorned style in which bare concrete constructions are the rule. De Beurs was an expressive building with 'aeroplane windows': windows with smoothly rounded corners and a bobbing crest at the top that were sunk into the facades in rows of four. The Aesthetics and Heritage Board labelled the demolition an 'irreparable mistake'.

44 Pon House

Rondebeltweg 31
QuA Associates
2008
Ruby van den Munckhof, Vincent Beekman (proj.)

Pon Holding's head office was inspired by classic country houses with a mid-section and wings, but also by aircraft carriers with long landing strips that run diagonally. All these elements were translated into a hovering construction with two wings and an entrance hall. An asphalt drive runs up from the road to the glass mid-section. From there, starting at a platform, two stairways provide access to the wings. At the front, the roof above the wings is supported by V-shaped columns that appear to be growing out of the concrete supports underneath the building. The front facade is partly made of Norwegian slate. The corners are kept transparent. The drive provides spaces for showcasing the models of the machines produced by Pon. At the back, narrow balconies stretch along the glass facade, which is reflected in a large pond that has a straight stone edge. Behind it is grass and a stand of willow trees. The facade at the back features a large, recessed space: a deep balcony where employees can take in the air. The railings have horizontal aluminium strips. Inside, many of the walls are made of floor-to-ceiling glass.

House Wine

With the changing climate, vines are advancing to the North. By now there are some two hundred vineyards in the Netherlands. These are not neatly aligned next to or opposite each other like on the Route des Grand Crus in Burgundy, but situated in rural places such as in Almere on Kemphaan and in Oosterwold. The wines of city vineyard Hof and wine house LCBT (Life Contains Beautiful Things) are delicious. Which goes to show that the grass isn't always greener on the other side of the hill.

45 Buitenkans (A Rare Opportunity)

Ambt Dorknoperlaan
Various architects
2007-2013
Renz Pijnenborgh, Peter van der Cammen, Frans van der Werf, Jaap van der Laan (proj.)

An eco-village, surrounded by woodland, with much greenery on the mostly communal grounds. Seven houses were built here on free plots. In addition, there are 48 timber frame units – some detached, some in small rows – in lively Scandinavian colours. The ground floor is plastered, the first floor is finished in colourful tongue-and-groove planking. The houses all have solar boilers, wall heating, excellent insulation, and green roofs. The rainwater flows to the central pond, which not only stores the water but is also a garden of delights for plants and animals. Parking is situated at the entrance, keeping the rest of the grounds car-free. The architects were inspired by Rudolf Steiner, the promoter of anthroposophical architecture, and by architect Ton Alberts, an advocate of oblique and round corners and lines based on natural forms. In spite of the great variety in translations of these principles that can be observed in De Buitenkans, the whole is still a unity, apart from a few detached villas with mismatched shapes and colours. In 2013 a community centre was added with a remarkable, crow's nest-like extension at the front.

A Cunning Plan

This project by the Collectief Particulier Opdrachtgeverschap (collective private commissioning) was started by a small group of environment-minded people and was completed successfully with the help of housing corporation De Alliantie. A minimum of 42 participants were needed for the initiative, but people would leave along the way. De Alliantie then took over twenty houses, guaranteeing a 'critical mass' and securing the financial basis for the project. To avoid unequal relationships in the decision-making process De Alliantie modestly occupied only one representative seat during building meetings.

46 Veranda Houses

Marten Toonderlaan
Onix architecten
2003-2006
Haiko Meijer (proj.)

Most people who happen to enter this small neighbourhood are surprised by the pleasant ambiance and the harmonious houses on the sloping green lawns. These are ten villas in the form of large wooden housing sheds, each of which contains three to five apartments. At one side, half underneath the houses, are the entrances, the storage spaces and parking places. At the other side, residents can enter the garden landscape around the houses straight from their living rooms. The proprietors have shared ownership of the gardens and also maintain them themselves. At the head side of the housing sheds the roofs protrude far out, adding a romantic element to the otherwise straight, modernistic design. The wooden facade cladding with the relief of vertically placed lattices softens the transition between nature and architecture. Here one feels what green quality in an urban environment can accomplish. The parklike garden layout, with planted islands and woodchips between the gravel and the grass, really make this a very lovely spot.

Almere Stories

In late 2023, Niña Weijers published *Cassandra*, the fourth book in the Almere Stories series. The project invites writers to come and live in Almere for a while and write a book based on their experiences. For her subject, Weijers took the disappearance of 17-year-old Cassandra van Schayk. After a night out in March 2007, Cassandra did not return home. Three weeks later her body was found in the local Noorderplassen. A cold case that perhaps can be reopened following Weijers' honest description, even though the lack of hard facts is a formidable hindrance.

47 Malmö Hüs

Macassarweg
Tjitte Tigchelaar
2005-2008

In 2007, Almere reserved a strip of three kilometres between the railroad and Evenaar for experimental building projects. One of the first of these was the Malmö Hüs, a square-shaped, timber frame, four-storey flat on a plinth of dark brickwork with four houses for disabled people.
The 52 apartments above can be accessed from galleries on the inner side of the building. The railings, alternated with vertical screens, look like they were drawn with a pencil. The fourth side consists of footbridges, the refined construction of which stands out against the sky. The yellow front doors form a nice contrast with the red cedar. The apartments have balconies on the outside. Only the uppermost floor has a closed facade, which provides a bold ending of the volume. The finishing with predominantly vertically placed wooden strips is nicely detailed. On the north side of the building bulges somewhat and the wooden strips are placed horizontally here. Here six business accommodations and eight studios are located. The architect found inspiration for this project at the 2001 building exposition BO01 in Malmö, where he studied the Swedish method of wooden constructions.
It seems fitting that the interior garden by bureau Zwaan is Scandinavian in atmosphere with birch trees, hills of ferns, and a wooden duckboard.

Open or Closed

A two-part bronze sculpture by Cor Litjens is the finishing touch of this place. The work consists of interior walls with framed door openings. Matter and space interact playfully here. On the wall is a poem by Bert Schierbeek:

A door is open
or closed

a door that is open
is a hole towards the space

a door that is closed is
part of the wall
it delineates the space

if it moves
it is a door

so am I
a door

48 Omar Ibn Al Khattab Mosque

Bintangweg 3
Gerard Rijnsdorp
2015

Walls of semi-transparent glass blocks rest on a brickwork base. The glass blocks feature a pattern of green and blue stones. Rows of vertical windows reach down into the base. The two minarets have a high brick base, supporting a pinnacle of silk-screened glass with a dome, crowned with a tower of copper spheres, the *jamour*. The minarets can be lighted from within, forming a beacon in the neighbourhood. The Arabic star motif on the glass is repeated in the glass entrance doors, skylights, and windows. The women enter at the front to reach their prayer room in the top of the building. On the floor below that is a similar room for the men. The two rooms are connected by a niche with a skylight that bulges out in the front facade; an architectural intervention to indicate the direction of Mecca. In addition to the prayer rooms there are many classrooms and a large meeting space with sofa's s against the walls. At the centre of the building is a square light court, like the ones in traditional dwellings in Morocco. All the corners of the building are rounded off. The combination of glass and brick makes it very expressive.

In Love

The band De Softies were real softies with lovely songs. They made 'twijfelpop' (doubt pop) with Dutch lyrics. You could say that bandleader Daniël van der Zee was Almere's first town troubadour. He can still be found in the shopping areas with his guitar. He writes all his own lyrics, which are often about episodes from his own life:

I fell in love with the prettiest girl in school
So things didn't look so bad at all yet
Oh my dear Almere
Living was something you had to learn
With your emptiness in the cold wind
You poor foundling

49 Park Strip Evenaar

Evenaar
Boto van der Meulen
2007-2013

The Evenaar is the backbone of Almere Buiten. A gently undulating course, reminding the pleasantly swaying motorist of the time that all this land was still water. In 2007 the wide central reservation between the lanes was redesigned by Boto van der Meulen. He transformed a 50-metre-wide no man's land into a three-kilometre-long park. One can experience the qualities realised here by following the winding path along seas of wildflowers grouped by colour on small hills.

The path also leads from one pavilion to another with small businesses such as an ice cream parlour, restaurant, and snack bar. Along the way are red 'cages' for various, clearly indicated sports: Tennis. Basketball. Skating. These are facilities that appeal to youngsters, who energise the hitherto dead strip with their inexhaustible energy. During this walk one may recognise a great number of trees, some of which have a Corten steel plate at their base with a punched-in poem by an Almerian poet.

Search and Find

Almere is rich in archaeological sites. Shipwrecks, arrow points, seeds, and a rare fish funnel from the stone age have been found here. Objects that tell us about how things once were. They are usually left in the ground, for the purpose of future research.
These sites cannot be developed and are often marked with works by artists. One important site lies a little to the north of Evenaar. Here, residents have created the VINDplaats (FINDplace) Zenit. It is a meeting point for the neighbourhood with historical huts, fireplaces, and a culture platform. The entrance is on the right of Borneostraat 3.

50 Denemarken (Denmark)

Chatelainestraat
Claus en Kaan
2006
Felix Claus, Katrin Weber (proj.)

These 26 semi-detached, two-storey starter homes are grouped along two V-shaped rows around an enclosed garden. They are supplemented with four apartments, located at the point of the V. There we also find the entrance door to the communal enclosed garden, where each dwelling has its own wooden deck. The back-doors were placed in the storerooms at the back, which have a saddleback roof and a porthole. The carcass of the houses is made of concrete and the front and back facades are clad in wood. The most striking aspect of this project are the deep red colour of the facades and the bright white frames around the windows and doors. These frames vary in height and width, thus forming separate, expressive elements. The use of wood, the red colours, the planting with small trees on mounds in the enclosed garden, are all reminiscent of Scandinavia. When in the next maintenance round the entire complex is painted in one go, the whole marring patchwork of differently faded tints of red will be remedied.

DIY

De Stripmaker is a pilot project of 27 houses built according to the Wikihouse principle; an affordable, very sustainable, freely available digital building system that provides DIY builders with everything they need to realise their own timber frame house. The house is designed and drafted in the system. A computer-aided milling machine cuts all the boards you need and the whole package is delivered on location. Then you start to build. In De Stripmaker the houses are still close together, but seeing the results triggers many people's imaginations. A system like a dream-machine.

51 Oostvaarderskliniek (Hospital)

Carl Barksweg 3
Studio M10
2005-2008
Martien Jansen (proj.)

In a forensic psychiatric hospital, prisoners with mental disorders receive therapy. Security is important here and this is why this type of building often has a closed appearance. Not here, though. By applying a special type of glass in combination with bars, the facade of the longitudinal building volume, which lies parallel to the street, looks quite transparent and is not out of tune with the houses in the vicinity. This part of the complex has an interior street with skylights, which provides access to the functional spaces on both sides. The doors and walls in this section have round windows, underlining the open character. In front of the rooms on the first floor a gallery was constructed, making the street more spacious. Behind this multi-tenant building is a large inner courtyard – not visible from the street – with housing units and single-storey workshops. The garden with straight strips and borders facilitates gardening, play, and sports. The whole is surrounded with a concrete wall with vertical cannelures. Right behind it strips of woodland were planted, so one hardly notices the wall from outside. In 2009, the Oostvaarderskliniek was chosen as BNA building of the year because of its innovative appliance of materials.

A-A-Almere

Black Pencil is an ensemble with an unusual line-up and a broad repertoire. Every year they present the A-A-Almere programme with music written by composers from Almere and dedicated to places in and around Almere. In 2023, for example, the programme featured a composition with a film by author and songwriter Jaco Benckhuijsen, who already followed the future route of the IJmeer connection by kayak.

52 Nature Experience Centre De Oostvaarders

Oostvaardersbosplaats 1
Drost + van Veen
2007-2008
Evelien van Veen (proj.);
Woonwerk Architecten (exp. 2024)

This centre was built to provide visitors with a view of the unique nature reserve at the eastern border of Almere, the Oostvaardersplassen, now part of Nieuw Land National Park. It is a higgledy-piggledy building that looks like a ship that has run aground on the edge of the dike. Black, contrasted by a bright green-yellow in the deeply recessed windows at the front, an ingenious way of making the building glow from within.
Once inside, visitors can lose themselves in the breathtaking view from a protruding balcony high up in the building. Binoculars are available, allowing them to zoom in on the birds and the large herbivores in this nature reserve. The room on the first floor provides information about flora and fauna and also houses an office and meeting space. Downstairs is a restaurant.
With the growing number of visitors, the Almere pavilion has become the major access point to the park, necessitating an expansion. The design for this is by Woonwerk Architecten, who focused on widening the existing building, mainly hidden inside the body of the dike.

Bull's-eye

The location of the Nature Experience Centre was originally reserved for extending the A3 from Nijkerk to Zaandam, but the unplanned development of the nature reserve led to a change in plans. People should really be given the opportunity to experience this wonderful area. Stad & Natuur (City & Nature), which managed the area, invited three firms for a tour and ask them to present a sketch design within two weeks. Evelien van Veen, who had just given birth, was given a report of the tour by her partner Simone Drost and purely from her imagination she sketched the winning design. One can also score a bull's-eye from a great distance.

53 BouwRAI 3 Eilandenbuurt

Architect Carel – later Carlos – Weeber, coined the term Het Wilde Wonen (Wild Living) in 1997. The Netherlands really wouldn't go to the dogs if everyone would be allowed to determine the shape of their own house, he said. This certainly caused a stir in the regulated world of construction where developers presumed to know exactly what the market demanded of them. Almere took up the gauntlet and organised a third BouwRAI exhibition under the title 'Het Gewilde Wonen' ('Desired Living'). Architectural firms and developers could submit proposals for carcass houses that future occupants would be allowed to detail at their own discretion. It was a method for exploring whether consumers wanted a bigger say in appearance, size, layout, and finishing of their homes. The city had just turned 25 and Almere was ready for a new experiment. A jury chose eleven projects that gave consumers many options. Often both layout and size of the houses could be adapted according to wish. Especially in the finishing much variation was possible. Although sales didn't always go smoothly, this BouwRAI marked the beginning of the development towards self-building that would strongly define Almere in the years to come.

53a Boiler Room Dwellings

Tahitistraat
Marlies Rohmer
1999-2001

These houses consist of two contrasting parts. There is a 'castle tower' with a coat of African slate, for stairwells, storage, sanitary facilities, and technical installations, that is connected to an industrial hall with aluminium strips in front of the windows, the height, width, and layout of which are flexible.

53b House Boats

Arubapier
Verheijen/Verkoren/Knappers/De Haan
1999-2001
Fons Verheijen (proj.)

Concrete barges of 18 by 5 metres were placed at the pier, each with only a three-storey 'starting tower' of 3 by 5 metres on the street side. It contained sufficient facilities to enable people to start building at their own discretion on the back part. DIYers went for it and an explosion of creativity followed. Not one boat is like any of the others. A great variety in roof shapes, materials, windows, and balconies demonstrate that people's wishes for living can indeed be very different.

53c Cat's Back Dwellings

Jamaicastraat
Laura Weeber
1999-2001

The name of these villas is derived from the segmented, arched roofs. They lie with their 'head' at the water. Occupants could opt for a terrace under the curved roof or for a larger living room. At the front the houses could be extended too. The light colours of the front facades held a great appeal for many, making them think of a Caribbean atmosphere.

53d Warehouses

Bonairepier
Maarten Min
1999-2001

Elaborating on the older type of warehouse, Maarten Min designed very spacious three-storey premises at Bonairepier. Occupants could arrange the open interior space fully in accordance with their own wishes and the builder executed their plan. Cladding the facade with hardwood on a base of dark brick was the architect's choice.

54 Regenboogbuurt (Rainbow District)

Spectrumdreef a.e.
Various architects
1992-1998
Hans Laumanns, Henk de Boer (urban planning), Alle Hosper (landscape), Floor van Dusseldorp (colour expert)

The Regenboogbuurt (the Rainbow District) owes its name to the colourful housing there, for which Floor van Dusselburg made the entire plan. He also designed the black fencing and was involved in making the planting scheme. The plants and trees in Regenboogbuurt are in optimum harmony with the colours of the houses, which really cover the entire spectrum. Sometimes in the plasterwork, sometimes in mineral paint. The various architects found inspiration at the Onkel Toms Hütte and Britz neighbourhoods of Berlin, designed by Bruno Taut in the 1930s. This is most evident in Terracottastraat, Scharlakenstraat and Siennastraat, where saturated reds and greens are combined with glistening cobalt blue, while frames and doors have bright yellow accents. On the west side of the neighbourhood villas and semi-detached dwellings were built. In Het Middenrif we find courtyard housing, a primary school, and a supermarket. The housing blocks around Parlemoervijver are painted in pastel shades. The Lage Vaartse Front has three housing courtyards. The neighbourhood is cut into by a green strip in the form of an elongated wedge of cake.
The 850 Japanese cherry trees along Spectrumdreef, whose pink blossom contrasts so nicely with the red walls in the flowering season, inspired residents to organising an annual cherry blossom celebration. In early spring, picnics are held under the trees when the blossom leaves come down like snowflakes and people ponder the brevity of life.

54a Klein India (Little India)

Hennahof
Liesbeth van der Pol
1994-1998

This project consists of 72 houses in the form of two square courtyards facing each other. One has facades in shades of yellow, pink, and orange, the other in shades of blue. They enclose a long narrow pond, at the end of which is a blue four-storey housing block on one side and a similar volume in red on the other. These 'palaces', crowned with wrap-around steel balconies, each contain three apartments. The architect designed the project after a visit to India, where she was moved by how the Taj Mahal was situated near mirroring water. The houses in the courtyards have pointed storage rooms at the back. These separate the gardens in a pleasant manner and provide much privacy. At the front the grounds are communal and residents take care of maintenance together.

54b Tower Houses

Chamoisstraat
Aldo van Eyck, Julyan Wickham
1996-1998

These houses, in bright yellow with blue window frames and soft orange side facades, have round towers at the front. Each tower contains a kitchen, a bedroom on the first floor, and on top of that a real tower chamber with access to a spacious roof terrace. The striking round head of the dwelling is at the tip of a triangular floor plan in which all spaces are fitted together in an ingenious manner. Garages with white doors connect the units.
The towers give the street an unparalleled rhythm. The association with castles pops up. The refined planting scheme with blossom trees is the finishing touch.

55 Rooie Donders (Red Rascals)

Pastelstraat
Liesbeth van der Pol
1994-1998

These eye catchers on the A6 motorway are the city's icons. When you see them, you know: this is Almere. The base of the towers consists of apartments that are like buttresses that support the flats above them. In these wide bases eight apartments were realised that enjoy a garden at ground level. The apartments are accessed via a footbridge. The buildings' silhouettes changes to a smaller profile at the eighth floor, in a tight rhythm.
The balconies provide lightness.
These three residential buildings marked a transition from the low-rise neighbourhoods of Almere to the polder landscape. Their shape refers to industrial buildings and electricity pylons, but also to grain silos. After all, the polder would become the grain silo of the Netherlands. Profiled steel sheets are framed by horizontal and vertical lines of cold-formed steel. The balconies are enveloped in red steel grilles as are the fences, chimneys, and window frames. Everything is red. This separates these buildings from 'traditional' construction and makes them compete with the surrounding landscape.
Above the base, each story contains three apartments, with penthouses making up the narrow top. The magnificent view of the polder and the orientation towards the sun are the penthouses' greatest asset.

Red

When Liesbeth van der Pol won the Jonge Maaskant Architecture Award in 1993, it opened new doors for her. Her fresh style of designing appealed to Almere's city council and they invited her for a commission in the Regenboogbuurt. A fine location with a view of the polder. A grand gesture in housing was called for here.
In her watercolour the three towers were initially yellow, blue, and red, but in the end the colour was decided by a bright red Kenzo suit that she triumphantly showed to the commissioners by taking off her raincoat.

56 Wooden Hotel

Trekweg 1
Sander Mirck
2019-2023

In 2019 the wooden restaurant Culinair Festijn (culinary fest) was opened near the entrance to Almere Buiten. It was built on piles made of the very solid laminated CLT wood. The roof's staggering zigzag line folds over a large hospitality space, presenting a striking facade to the nearby roundabout. The protruding unit that contains the entrance is kept open at the front and has open stairs. Cars can park underneath the restaurant. In 2023, two freestanding, straight units with hotel rooms were added behind the restaurant.

Part of the original building was also transformed into hotel accommodation. With a total of 330 rooms, this budget hotel can accommodate a lot of overnight guests. The later buildings, of four stories each, are made of prefab modules, also in CLT. All rooms have double doors that open up to the galleries around the blocks. Between the two straight new volumes and the 2019 building situated obliquely to them, an inner garden was created. Together, the three buildings look like a facility that can accommodate people for many years to come.

Elephants

Since 2000, the Elephants stand where the A6 and A27 motorways meet at the Almere junction. Five slow beasts by artist Tom Claassen, who also made figures of men out of tree trunks in Almere Buiten. Their simplified form – they have no tusks and their trunks are truncated – is similar to the models for toy elephants you can saw together from pieces of leather. One can still see the stitches. Claassen thinks the location is very apt: 'Hannibal crossed the Alps with them and then you automatically end up at Almere Buiten.'

57a Havenkom met Gooizicht (Inner Harbour with Gooizicht)

Sluiskade
Adriaan van Erk
1989-1990

Almere Haven had to be a real harbour, since Dirk Frieling had decided upon this name for this part of the city.
To realise this harbour, the straight dike near the centre was interrupted and diverted. This created an inner harbour with one section for larger ships and a marina. The Gooizicht building, with many hospitality facilities in the plinth and apartments on top, embraces the inner harbour in a grand gesture. The complex forms a continuous wall on top of the new dike, with just a few passages to the parking lot behind it. The pitched roof is constantly interrupted by higher facade elements with white frames at the top. The lower apartments have semicircular balconies.
At Kruisstraat are two distinctive towers with a series of stacked round balconies placed on pillars in front of the building volume. The towers function as a kind of gate building pointing the way to the town centre behind it. In 2023, the well-known Van Rossems visited Almere for their television show, discussing what the young city had to offer. Sis van Rossem acknowledged the quality of the towers, whereas Maarten van Rossem launched into a rant against the Golvend Land (Undulating Land) complex at the edge of Gooimeer lake, which consists of a restaurant, a lower part with 75 apartments, and a 19-storey high-rise. Seated by the quay side, they dissed the tower in unison. In their view, it 'killed' the view. The lower volume was compared to a crematorium. 'May I call for its demolition?'

57b Golvend Land (Undulating Land)

Veerkade
Gert-Jan Hendriks
1999-2000

The elongated residential complex Golvend Land is a constellation of five vertical volumes of dark brick, with deeper lying horizontal and light-tinted building volumes leaning against them. There, glass is favoured and the occupants enjoy spacious roof terraces. On the adjacent green pier stands a residential tower. From the terraces at the front and back these apartments provide a panoramic view. Between two parts that jut out the stairwell with lift shaft is situated, which connects two apartments on each floor. The side facades are clad in dark brick. All apartments have three horizontal windows on that side.
The tower has turned out pretty substantial, but looks slender because of the clever use of materials. The low, square restaurant Bakboord has wide terraces on the waterfront at two sides.

57c Kerkgracht

Kerkgracht
Apon, Van den Berg, Ter Braak, Tromp
1974-1979
Dick Apon (proj.)

A shallow canal, fringed with lime trees, separates the two sides of the street. The brick facades with concrete courses have adornments on top that are reminiscent of the stepped gables of traditional canal houses. At ground level on the canal side the apartments are combined with shops. Some of these have an artistic slant, referring to the time that the idea was to make this an 'art canal'. The other side of the street has apartments only. Apon have deliberately used historicising elements to make the new residents feel at home. On the side of the market is an artwork of a dolphin on a table, by Marcel Smink. This peaceful animal marks the place where all Almerians gather on May 4 to commemorate the victims of World War II.

58 Signal Tower

Havenhoofd 134
Leendert Boer
1958

This tower was designed by a civil engineer, but it makes an architecturally harmonious whole. The circular disc on top is the roof, which doubles as a table for the radar equipment. The second disc hangs like a balcony around the white-plastered tower shaft itself, which has just one steel door. Behind it a spiral staircase leads to the tower room with windows all around, providing a view to all sides. The roof is supported here by slant trestles, forming a gradual transition to the tower shaft.

This signal tower once stood near Wijk bij Duurstede to guide the shipping traffic at the crossing between the Lek river and the Amsterdam-Rhine canal. On the occasion of the twentieth anniversary of the city, the Department of Waterways donated the tower to Almere, hoping of course that this special building would be preserved here. Which it was, and in 2022 it was placed on the list of municipal monuments. The signal tower has been in use as a B&B since 2019.

Name

In 1958, the western part of Zuidelijk Flevoland was designated as overflow area for the Randstad and as agricultural land. The first Structure Plan for the Zuidelijke IJsselmeerpolder from 1961 indicated the location where the new city, which would be named IJmeerstad or Zuidweststad, would be built. Wim Otto, one of the two leaders of RIJP, proposed the name Almere, after Almaere, as the area was called before it was named Zuiderzee. So, Almere it was. In Almaere were two large islands: Schokland and Urk.

59 De Werven (The Home Zones)

Schoolwerf a.e.
Joop van Stigt
1974-1977

These first Almerian dwellings are of the type we now call retro-architecture, or in less friendly terms, 'new bourgeois architecture', a school in architecture that favoured the small scale and cosiness. Children should be able to play safely in the streets and a diverse range of people should be able to live together there. The result was Het Woonerf (The Home Zone), the ultimate answer to the demand for a safe and varied living environment. A courtyard with greenery at the centre and houses around it, child-friendly and with sufficient parking space. No through traffic is allowed here and the density of the built environment facilitates contact among residents. Van Stigt designed groups of 20 to 25 dwellings on square plots with bevelled corners. At one location they are grouped like a cloverleaf around a square with trees. A bit further on, the courtyards are more loosely situated. 26 types of dwelling were realised. Storerooms, loggias, and outside stairs are different everywhere, although indoor stairs, kitchens, and sanitary elements are mostly the same. This allowed for very fast building, as people were desperate for living space at the time. When visiting De Werven now, 40 years later, we see a successful, varied neighbourhood where the blue roofs and doors form a fine contrast against the now mature greenery.

Murder in Almere Haven

When his father was arrested for murdering two children in Amsterdam, Paul Spruit was still in his early teens. The Spruit family in Almere Haven had nothing to do with it, but received severe threats all the same. At her wit's end, Paul's mother took in her violent ex-husband again, who also assaulted Paul. His reports to the police yielded no results and in a terrible moment Paul stabbed and killed his stepfather. Crime reporter Peter R. de Vries wrote a book about the case, which was adapted for the screen in 2023. Was Paul a victim of circumstance or could he have chosen differently?

60 Corrosia

Markt 1
Rob Blom van Assendelft, Jan Koning
1974-1979

The multifunctional Corrosia, designed as a prelude to a city hall to be developed behind it, has a broad interior street that should have opened onto a bridge to that new building. This street is still the heart of the interior, giving access to the theatre, library, restaurant, exhibition hall and spaces to relax. Some flats for young people have a private entrance. Two continuous rooflights jut out above the building, which takes its name from its facades made of strips of Corten steel, a material whose outer layer corrodes to a distinctive rust-brown colour.
The 2012 renovation by Rik Lagerwaard added two towers and replaced the closed plinth at the front with glass. With that, the murals depicting episodes of the city's history by artist Nanne Balyon disappeared.
The layout with interconnected user spaces and split-level floors has been retained. Corrosia remains a landmark on the market square, still fully living up to its social and cultural function.

Acrobat

Een Beeld (a sculpture) by Paul de Reus was revealed in 2009. It was a gift from the city to Jan de Vletter, who had retired as director of a housing corporation in 2007. His directorship was characterised by a great sensitivity for the residents and a special eye for art in public space. The city of Almere honoured years of dedicated work by letting him choose the artist. The bronze sculpture shows an acrobat holding a ball with some hundred faces up in the air. It symbolises the way in which Jan had fulfilled his task all those years.

61 De Goede Rede Church

Kerkgracht 60
Gerrit Steen
1977-1979

The main hall of ecumenical church centre De Goede Rede has a hypar-shaped roof. On one side, the space is 21 metres high. On the opposite side 14 metres. In between, a wood-clad ceiling curves gracefully from one point to the other. On the tallest side is a vertical opening in the wall in which square concrete blocks hang at equal distances from each other. Rays of light fall in between the blocks. They are white on the inside, dark on the outside and they hold together the outer walls that have uneven heights at that corner. A stained-glass window with a dashing, upward motif injects colour into the interior. The chapel located on the other side of the wide entrance hall has a rounded structure with windows in the drum. At the rear is a series of multi-functional rooms. A Lady Chapel was added during renovation in 2005. The striking 35-metre-high tower, which stands apart from the main building like a campanile, consists of four vertical brick sections with white concrete elements between them, suggesting a strong upward movement. Once a week, the city carillonneurs play the carillon.

Goede Rede Concerts

Right from the start, in addition to services by various denominations, concerts and other events took place here, including fashion shows, musicals, and flea markets, as had been the intention of architect Gerrit Steen. There is a bar and there are rooms with a living room atmosphere where elderly people meet on a weekly basis. The main hall has wonderful acoustics, which inspired Wilma Hartsuiker in 2015 to set up a platform for classical music with a varied, high-quality programme.

It is this robust cultural function that helped the listing of the church as a municipal monument in 2024.

62 Tuinhuis (Garden House)

Leemwierde 213-239
Korthtielens
2012-2018
Gus Tielens (proj.)

Many senior citizens, the pioneers of yesteryear, would like to stay in Haven. To encourage them to leave their single-family homes, the Garden House with 27 social rental flats was built. Urban densification in the predominantly 'village-like' Haven was most welcome. It brought metropolitan allure to the neighbourhood, executed with architectural beauty and a good level of detail.
The architects prove that a building made of old-fashioned gravel concrete can in fact be charming. Washed concrete has been given a modern twist and offers surprising solutions. Consistently carried through in the support elements, floating balcony corners and rounded shapes, it pleases the eye. Minimum footprint combined with maximum freedom. Each room opens onto the wraparound balcony. The building has a concrete, self-supporting structure of terraces and is clad in wood. The columnar form is reflected in balcony storage units, niches and planters.
The residents are responsible for minor maintenance, management and cleaning, thus retaining control over their living environment.
The interior has stylistic elements reminiscent of the Amsterdam School. The colour palette of soft yellow railings, black tiling and panelling and grey ceilings with sound-absorbing paper cellulose are stylish. By contrast, the typography is twenty-first-century: giant numbers identify the flats.

Winner

Het Tuinhuis won the Almere Architecture Award in 2018. One of the jury members was Titia Frieling, pictured in the front here. She was one of the initiators of the De Fantasie 25, De Realiteit 39, and Eenvoud 38 competitions. Her sharp mind and eye for quality have helped Almere to make a name for itself. Titia was also one of the driving forces behind the Museumbos 91. She is an artist, and the widow of the project leader of Projectburo Dirk Frieling, one of the godparents of Almere, who died in 2011. In 2017, Titia received the badge of honour from the city.

63 De Spiegel (The Mirror)

Houtstraat 1-79
Santman van Staaden
2010

This complex of four maisonettes and forty private sector rental flats consists of three vertical units separated by transparent staircases. In the silhouette, the end of the front unit on Houtstraat stands out. This takes the form of a glass house with a gabled roof. A house that seems to extend into the high glass plinth in the end facade, which recedes behind angled, steel columns. These support the cantilevered five-storey middle section of this unit, which is clad in brick. The middle volume also has a gabled roof. There, seven floors have a brick mantle surrounding a green core, which continues into the plinth of the front section. The rear building section is enveloped entirely in brick. It has a flat roof and balconies with green-tinted glass at the back. On one side, the structure with orange balconies also projects sideways. The volumes of the three units are interwoven both horizontally and vertically through ingenious use of materials and colours and appear to slope upwards towards the back. A highly plastic building that effectively plays with the visual effects of material, colour and shape.

Boulevard

It took some getting used to for the residents of Almere Haven when the road along the inner harbour was changed into a low-traffic boulevard. The distance from West to East became quite a bit longer for motorists. The many cafés and restaurants expanded their outdoor areas, catering more and more to cyclists and walkers enjoying the view of the long wooden pier and the boats mooring there. The modernist pavilion of Michelin-star restaurant Bij Brons is an eyecatcher on the eastern side. De Harmonie,

situated on the western side in the long facade of Gooizicht, is a cosy Almerian meeting point.

64 Centraal Wonen (Central Living)

Hoekwierde
Thijs Gerretsen
1984
Jurgen van Staaden (ren. 2010)

Twenty homes of different sizes are situated in a strip on a high embankment. They have white window frames and bright blue doors and wooden cladding. You reach the lower units via a flight of steps and enter the house through a courtyard. First-floor units have an external steel staircase with a narrow lean-to-roof. In front of the row of houses is a street and along it a picking garden and a series of buildings for collective use. There is a living room with a fireplace, a kitchen and guest rooms. There are DIY spaces, a place for washing machines, and a communal terrace. Some residents have studios there. On the architect's initiative, the complex was made part of housing corporation Ymere. He wanted to realise it in social rent, so that the less fortunate could also move into the complex.
It turned out to be a golden formula. The complex, based on the ideals for central living from the 1970s, has been thriving for forty years. The houses are close to a green common with old poplars and the full length of the rear side is adjacent to a bird-rich grove visited and maintained by all neighbourhood residents. This also fosters neighbourhood-wide social cohesion.

Murals

The idea of documenting local history in murals came from housing corporation De Groene Stad. In 2001, a delegation had visited the French city of Lyon, where many facades are painted. Unfortunately, not enough care was taken in preparing the surfaces, causing the painted layers of plaster to start peeling beyond repair. Sometimes, murals would fall prey to renovations, as in the case of Corrosia. Others were vandalised. The eyes of the gents sitting at the bar in Café De Burgemeester were stabbed out many times. Luckily, by now street art artists have been leaving their colourful mark on public space everywhere in the city.

65 Senior Care Home De Overloop

Boogstraat 1-143
Herman Hertzberger
1980-1984

De Overloop senior care home is built of grey concrete brick with white window frames divided into squares and rectangles, parting the facades in long strips. Conservatories have been installed on the road and garden sides, hanging from the facades like boxes over two floors. The building has several wings that fold around an inner garden with a pond. On three sides, it is bordered by low-rise service flats. The four-storey entrance combines round and straight forms, deep communal balconies and, on the ground floor, a small bay window. On the first floor above the entrance is a restaurant. At this spot, the second and third floors have entresols, from which you can see into the restaurant. Herman Hertzberger is known as a structuralist architect. A movement in which buildings are designed as structures that are meant to encourage encounters. In De Overloop, there were therefore many benches in the corridors. The top half of the front doors could be opened separately, allowing residents to have contact with each other. These typical elements disappeared when the building was renovated in 2019. The window overlooking the corridor from the units remained, as did the many balconies and seating areas by the stairwells.

White Concrete Stone

Architect Herzberger opted for a light concrete stone, clearly against the wishes of Almere Haven's project leader Hans Laumanns, who wanted everything 'slant and brown', because it would make Almerians feel more at home. Laumanns later commented: 'He taunted me by making the plan completely specified. If I asked him what material he was going to use for the facades, he would say that he hadn't decided yet. Later it turned out that he had secretly obtained

the building permit with grey-white concrete stone!'

66 Police Station

Bivak 1
OMA
1982-1985
Rem Koolhaas (proj.)

This building, the first design by Rem Koolhaas ever executed, was designated a municipal monument in 2019.
The elongated facade consists of a wall that stands as a loose element in front of the building volume, executed in smooth blue brick. The glass entrance protrudes slightly and is flanked by a slab of composite material, which over time has changed colour from pink to grey. The rest of the building was done in white-painted brick with an anthracite plinth. All windows are horizontal in shape and have black aluminium frames, with originally blue vertical slats on the inside to keep out the sun. At the rear facades, cantilevered aluminium grilles with sun protection strips are placed above the windows, accentuating the horizontal lines of the structure. The second floor occupies only the middle section and rises above the flat roof of the ground floor with two volumes. On one of the short sides is a tall garage with rolling door. Behind a fence attached to it, you can see the service entrance and parking spaces. This well-balanced but somewhat 'safe' building does not yet show traces of the later Koolhaas who found drama essential in building.

Right of Way

Pedestrian crossings in rainbow colours are a common occurrence in many European cities. They draw attention to accepting lesbians, gays, bisexuals, and transgenders. In late 2019, Almere too got such an inclusive crossing, right in front of the Flevo hospital. Simultaneously, a 'transcrossing' or LHBTQ+-crossing as they are usually called nowadays, was installed, the first one in Europe! The colours pink, light blue and white refer to the transgender flag. The message is clear: in Almere there's room for everyone.

67 Upcycle Centre

De Steiger 113
LKSVDD architecten
2017-2020
Ronald Olthof, Arent Kappelhoff, Chester Rijders, Radboud Seckel (proj.)

The municipality of Almere aspires to be a city without waste in the future and is therefore investing in new concepts. With the Growing Green City idea in mind, this upcycle platform has been realised. The exterior wall with a vertical timber structure houses small businesses in the plinth. The material was harvested from demolished municipal property and felled trees. Other materials came from a demolished neighbouring sports hall and swimming pool. Ceiling panels, door handles and benches from the changing rooms were also reused. Upon entering, motorists are directed to the first floor. Containers on the ground floor collect waste material. The walls of the concrete core on the ground floor divide the spaces for offices and storage. The main office is located on the first floor. A striking feature is the floating roof: it is fitted with solar panels and collects rainwater used to flush the sanitary facilities and clean the grounds. The steel columns and beams again come from previously demolished structures. They can be recognised by their anthracite colouring, while new steel components are grey in colour. The building is fully dismountable and movable. Everything is screwed down and can therefore be unscrewed.

BOT

Every year, the Stichting Behoud Oude Technieken (preserve traditional techniques) organises open days to demonstrate old machines and other historical objects. No upcycling here! On the contrary, the foundation's aim is to show how things were originally made and teach younger generations what life looked like in days gone by. The foundation is located in Almere and used to organise the Steam Festival. That festival has stopped but the torch is carried on by the BOT foundation, which enjoys great interest.

68 Sheep Barn

Muiderweg 8
70F architecture
2007
Bas ten Brinke (proj.)

In 2006, building the Eksternest (Magpie's Nest) in the Vroege Vogelbos (Early Bird Forest) was sold to Triade, a care organisation, which established catering facilities there. The proceeds were used to build a sheep barn next to it for the flock of around a hundred sheep of Stad & Natuur, the institution responsible for nature education in the city. It became an understated building, consisting of a steel skeleton clad with bevelled wooden boards. The shape of the long hall is kept low on one side and springs up from the ground on the other. The barn thus consists almost entirely of roof, just like the traditional type of sheep barn. A dormer has been added to the front section. Utility spaces have been fitted in there: an office, sanitary facilities, a residence for the shepherd, as well as the shop of the Almeerse Wolunie, which relocated here and shares knowledge about wool. Halfway up the structure, a deep-set panoramic window has been installed to allow interested children to look inside. The curved shape of the stable grounds the building in a positive sense.
The design won one of the prizes at the World Architecture Festival in Barcelona in 2008.

A Sheep...

The flock of Stad & Natuur is made up of four old breeds of sheep. Their most important task is to stop the advance of the giant hogweed in the Vroege Vogelbos. They eat the buds, so no flowers and seeds are formed and the plant no longer spreads. This is very necessary as this invasive species threatens to supplant indigenous plants everywhere in Almere. The Wolunie gathers the sheep's wool to process it with traditional methods and develop new products.

69 De Marken

Redemark a.e.
Ben Loerakker
1977-1979

There was once a cooperative housing association in Almere Haven, the CWAH, which wanted to develop a safe, social and pleasant living environment for people regardless of their income or education. The association set up an administrative structure, made a plan and boldly hired an architect. Ben Loerakker designed a street with a double row of houses on each side, facing each other with their gardens. The street ends in a circular lawn on which another twelve houses are located. A shed and a neighbourhood meeting place, both communally owned, tell of the original concept, focused on contact and community. A number of houses on the lawn have an extra floor on top. Many people have deviated from the original colours of white and blue for the doors and window frames, but in the wider part of the street, which also has trees, one can still clearly see how it was once intended. The side walls of the two houses at the beginning of the street are finished with angled wooden slats, surrounding a rectangular brick plane. The second floor of both protrudes forward, creating a gateway giving access to the neighbourhood.

Splinter Plastic

One of the things Almere does in terms of sustainability is appointing climate mayors. Chris Soebroto is one of them. He goes everywhere to explain what may happen and what we can do to prevent it. He was present at the award ceremony of the Stop Plastic Waste Pin in 2024, an initiative of the Almerian Rotary clubs. The pin was presented to the Dronten firm Flestic by the winner of 2023: the Flevoziekenhuis, which succeeded in drastically reducing the huge amounts of hospital waste by applying a clever waste separation system.

70 Cemetery

Oosterdreef 15
Christian Zalm
1976-1980

Almere's first cemetery is bordered by the Gooimeerdijk and the Oosterdreef. It consists of burial plots in scattered chambers on mounds. In fact, the clay soil had to be raised with sand to provide a moisture-permeable final resting place. The rooms are shaped like water lily leaves and bordered by thick hedges of native plant species such as lime and hawthorn. Towards the dike, the mounds get higher, creating a natural transition to the road above. Pedestrian and cycle paths meander freely through the park-like layout. Those who don't want to, need not see the graves behind the hedges. Entering the chambers through the wooden gates, one sometimes finds neat rows of graves, other times monuments scattered randomly in the grass. In terms of layout, some fields come close to the ambience of natural burial cemeteries, where the terrain indicates where the graves may be placed and there are no paths along rows of graves. In the chambers there are only tall trees, no shrubs. Designed by city architect Tjitte Tigchelaar, the auditorium was commissioned in 1979. The entire cemetery is on the list of possible municipal monuments.

Fare Well

Philippe van Thiel (1958-2021) was a well-known resident of Almere who ran the popular Haddock bar-restaurant with a marina and holiday cottages on the Weerwater. When he had to leave the spot because of the Floriade, a tough conflict with the municipality ensued. Philippe wanted to stay and be part of the event, but this didn't work out. When he suddenly died of cardiac arrest in 2021, it was immediately associated with the conflict. On his grave a steel ship sails into the unknown on a blue wave.

71 Bivouac

Meentweg 2 (Tuinpark Water-Land)
Rijksdienst voor de IJsselmeerpolders
1975

This small building was originally part of a group of eight units, each consisting of two prefab homes linked together. The group stood on the barren plain where the centre of Almere Haven 57 would later be built. The interior space was eleven by six metres, with a barn at right angles to it measuring six by three. There was a bathroom with a bathtub, an open kitchen with an extractor fan, and each dwelling had two bedrooms. Tenants were three State Police officers, two utility workers, two ambulance workers and the caretaker of the wooden building De Haak (The Hook) with their families. A total of thirteen adults and nine children. They had a tough time living here. They were faced with infestations of field mice, sandstorms and roaring excavators. The children went to school in Muiderberg, where the residents also did their shopping. It was not until 30 November 1976 that the first stone houses on the Schoolwerf could be moved into and Het Bivak (The Bivouac) could be vacated. The story goes that the civil service donated this specimen to Garden Park Water-Land around 1978, where it remained in use as an office and was well maintained. In 2023, it became a municipal monument on the grounds of 'its identity and experiential value'. As such, this unique piece of Almere history continues to tell the story of the earliest days.

The First One

On 3 November 1976, Henk and Lia de Klerk were handed the key of their new brick house as the official first residents of Almere. However, the very first Almerian was police officer Wim Leeman. He moved to Almere in 1975 to supervise the developing city and the rest of the impoldered land, together with two colleagues. He was assigned Bivak nr. 2. He was only allowed to live there for two and a half years, but he has kept the name sign and house number all his life, as well as an aerial photograph of the eight houses in the plane of sand. Jak Boumans has written his biography *De Allereerste Almeerder* (the very first Almerian). It recounts many interesting stories from those early days.

72 City Estate Kemphaan

Kemphaanpad 10
Bureau Nieuwland
1991-
Kees Hund (proj.)

The development of the estate began tentatively with places for organic gardening from an outdoor centre left over when the Almeerderhout woodlands had been planted. In 1991, they decided to turn it into a city estate. Kees Hunt designed a straight rectangle of wide ditches, with a multifunctional building in the centre. On its south side are two islands on which old monkeys from the AAP Foundation are allowed to roam. A formal section follows on the other side, bordered by double beech hedges on raised embankments. The paths in this section are straight as arrows. From the building, a long line of sight extends to a wilder part of the estate, where you can explore and wander. There is a maze and a replica of an old sheep barn. In the woodland surrounding the formal middle section, a variety of functions have been added, making the estate attractive to the public. Kindervakantieland (kids holiday land) is located here, a nature campsite, and the special hotel-lodge Het Groene Geheim. There is a biodynamic farm and inside a large greenhouse is a jungle garden with play areas for children. The AAP Foundation has two shelters here and the state forestry commission has a robust wooden structure with a café and shop near the popular climbing forest Fun Forest. Part of the surrounding woods have been laid out as an open-air museum for all tree species found in the polder. De Kemphaan has become a pleasure garden, where the connection between city and nature is experienced wherever you go.

73 Five-in-one Villa

Echobos 28
Next Architects
2007-2008
Michel Schreinemachers, Bart Reuser, Marijn Schenk (proj.)

In the Overgooi district, with a lot of private commissions, the bright orange Villa van Vijven (Five-in-one Villa) attracts a lot of attention. This villa was commissioned by a residents' collective consisting of five families. All the different living preferences have been realised in the design. There are five residential units on the first and second floors and an underlying square on the ground floor. Each house has two living levels perpendicular to each other. This Rubik's cube has been ingeniously designed to make the most of site-specific qualities. Each property has views of both the Gooimeer lake and the extensive gardens. The quarter-turn creates a special spaciousness and gives each home a double orientation: on the first floor east-west, creating a connection between street and garden; on the second floor north-south, making optimal use of the views and sunlight. By lifting the ground level on the spacious 5,000 m² plot, it has become a compact yet spacious design on the dike. The orange colour of the villa provides a powerful contrast to the blue skies and green nature and gives the building a distinctive, individual identity.

Gouden Piramide
Rijksprijs voor inspirerend opdrachtgeverschap

Gold

In 2007, the Villa van Vijven was nominated for the Golden Pyramid, the State award for inspiring commissionership.

Blue Green

> *In about a hundred years, the building of Almere will have become history, just like the Beemster and Schermer polders are now an essential part of Dutch history. Will Almere then be part of the canon of creating new land and new communities?*
>
> Jan de Vletter

With an area of nearly 25,000 hectares, Almere is a large municipality. 52 per cent of it consists of water. This does not only include the central lake, the Weerwater 24, the Lepelaarsplassen and the Noorderplassen 37, but also part of the Gooimeer and to the north and east part of the Markermeer. Scattered along the 42-kilometre coastline and inland bodies of water are beaches and marinas, and on Noorderplassen many homes have their own moorings. Water recreation has become part of Almere's DNA. We owe Weerwater to urban planner Teun Koolhaas, who considered blue as necessary for a healthy city as green. He fought hard to turn the just-reclaimed land into water again, hence the name Weer-water: Again-water. If anything, the story of the green is even more spectacular. In the first years after reclamation in 1968, 4,000 hectares of land were planted with large machines, first with reeds and rapeseed and then with native trees and shrubs. Eighty hectares remained farmland. Then there are also the parks and green wedges in built-up areas. Invariably, the planting of greenery preceded construction, so that there was landscaping and shelter everywhere. When Oosterwold 92 was created in the agricultural area next to the A27 motorway, the new residents were obliged to take on the green landscaping themselves and live up to the principle of 'Connect City and Nature'. Some robust but, in terms of planting, very varied strips were created. Kromslootpark, Beginbos and Vroege Vogelbos connect to Weerwater and the large Waterlandsebos and Cirkelbos, only to stop at the A27. To the north, the rich strip of woodland that will separate Poort and Pampus runs into the Noorderplassen and the wet grasslands below the Oostvaardersdijk. These large areas are connected to the greenery around and in the nuclei so that everyone can enjoy this enormous luxury.

The area where Oostvaardersplassen were formed was reserved for businesses. It remained untouched for years, to be used in due course. Initially, the only investment was in planting reeds and riparian crops, resulting in an unparalleled nature area for the city. It is largely on Lelystad territory, but its location on the western side of the province made Almere the place where the nature reserve could be used for recreation.
The more the city matures, the more you can see the value of the original development vision. More and more functions such as allotments, playgrounds and sports areas, restaurants and campsites are settling here. City and nature fuse and enrich each other. The ideal has become reality.

74 Villa Haumann Commandeur

Helenusstraat 14
Haumann Commandeur Architecten
2009-2010

On the eastern edge of the Homeruskwartier, an area was reserved to build architect-designed villas. On this challenging, triangular plot, the client wanted plenty of outdoor space. The set-back base of black brick created extra space for the garden, which covers half the plot. The first and second floors are for living and sleeping. The result is a house with a double veranda, referring to the verandas in Surinam, where the clients have roots. On the first floor, a large, free-hanging balcony, realised with a steel structure, leads to the garden.

On the street side, a curved panoramic window provides views of the park and the villas on the other side of the canal. The colour scheme, soft and hard yellow combined with black, again refers to sunny Suriname. The closed facades on the street sides are screened with a continuous, horizontal slatted strip. Behind these are four bedrooms. The second-floor bathrooms are characterised by the vertical facade finish, which provides privacy and visually breaks up the facade. The rounded corners create a soft profile.

Almere Bashing

From the very start, Almere fell prey to what we nowadays call Almere bashing. For instance, *Elseviers Magazine* wrote in 1979: 'And then there is the architecture of this would-be city. Small houses like mushrooms. Perhaps the regulations can make wearing pointed hats compulsory. Almere will be the laughingstock of architecture .... The sandbox of the new frumps. Just look at the tiny canal with small houses inspired by the seventeenth century. One could be forgiven for taking it for a cowboy village in some amusement

park. Kitsch elevated to the status of architecture.'

DIY Construction

People make the city.

Almere Principle nr.7

'Why is it that you can choose everything in your life, from school to partner, to work, but not the house you live in?' These were the words of Adri Duivesteijn, councillor from 2006 to 2013, when he launched his plans for more self-built houses in Almere. Not only people with money had to be given that opportunity, those who were dependent on corporations and property developers also had to be given a say in housing development. At that time, Almere had already conducted important experiments with DIY construction with De Fantasie 25 and De Realiteit 39. Fantasy could become reality if you gave people room to manoeuvre and adjusted regulations.

Architecture and urban planning are rightly considered expert disciplines, which require knowledge. But that does not mean that users cannot have much more input in the building process, and architects can be subservient and supportive rather than patronising and decisive. Almere picked up on the trend around 2000 with Gewilde Wonen 53 in the Eilanden neighbourhood, a variation on architect Carlos Weeber's Wild Living, who wasn't afraid of the chaos predicted if people made their own decisions.

In the Eilanden neighbourhood, residents' wishes were addressed, as many different choices were offered. For the Homeruskwartier in Poort, they took things a step further. Here, half of the homes were developed by residents and their advisers themselves. Additional incentives were provided with the 'I build affordably in Almere' scheme. Next came the collective variant. This involved groups of people putting their heads together and combining resources to realise their housing dreams. The results can even be found in upscale Overgooi. Oosterwold 92 became the pinnacle. Here, people could not only decide how they wanted to live, but also the construction of roads and paths, energy supply and water management were left to the residents themselves. Of course, there were rules here too. People were required to use a large part of the plot for urban agriculture and publicly accessible greenery, and no fences were allowed. A percentage for 'red' (the part that could be built on) was set for each type of plot. Much deliberation was needed to determine the layout and type of streets, and soon enough some enforcement was needed to make sure everyone followed the rules. Thus, the 4,300 hectares of Oosterwold were laid out with great freedom. They now show what a new kind of organic urbanism looks like, where individual expression is also allowed in architecture. Nowadays, there is no self-respecting city in the Netherlands where a number of plots are not cleared for DIY-construction. Almere has shown the way.

75 Het Klokhuis

Dettifosspad 7
Jord den Hollander and five children
2010-2011

The 'Design your dream house' competition, organised to mark the 25th anniversary of the children's programme Het Klokhuis, yielded 1,200 entries. As it turned out, children were very concerned with the climate, the environment and sustainability. What should the outside look like? How do you want to sleep, eat, and play? The five winners worked with architect Jord den Hollander on a model incorporating their ideas, resulting in a pink cake presented on a hand. The television programme followed the construction every week.
Their designs included sleeping under the sea, stargazing through the water in the 'Opsekopse huisje' (upside-down house), a toilet that flushes with rainwater, and a kitchen in the shape of a snail, because slow cooking is better than fast food. A slide to the outside illustrates the effect of gravity, and a round triple glass facade that can be unfolded like a harmonica takes you to the balcony that is exactly at sea level.
Every element of the house contains educational aspects, making it a popular place for special birthday parties and school visits. Here, building, housing and healthy living are in the spotlight, playfully integrating sustainability into everyday life.

What's in a name?

The address of the Klokhuis probably does not mean much to children. Few people will know that Dettifoss is one of the three waterfalls on Iceland. The street names in the Stripheldenbuurt (cartoon characters neighbourhood), though, will mean more to them. Who wouldn't want to live in the Brommy & Tommy Street, on Donald Duck Ave or at Catootje Path?

76 Paint it Red!

Beneluxlaan, Zwitserlandpad, Duitslandstraat
Kuiper Compagnons
2005-2010
Reinald Bosman (proj.)

The complex is located on a triangular plot, amid mainly rectangular plots. The Zwitserlandpad, a cycle and footpath, marks one of the sides of the triangle and cuts across the octagonal grid. This creates one route directing slow traffic to and from the avenues and Cascadepark.
The robust residential building has five floors and houses 22 flats for first-time buyers. Behind a protruding wall sculpture on Beneluxlaan is the entrance, which provides access to living rooms with floor-to-ceiling sliding glass doors. By placing the stairwell and bicycle storage on the inside, the balconies on that side could be stacked, while they are staggered on the other facade for a playful effect. The narrow end facade has high, double windows, making the building appear higher than it actually is.
The repetition of vertical accents contributes to the quirky and contemporary look of the building, which can be described as 'LEGO-like'. This colourful and dynamic design adds spice to the neighbourhood and offers a novel, modern housing solution for first-time buyers.

No Wallflower

The walls of Paint it Red! have plenty of character. Which couldn't be said of the walls of the buildings on the industrial zone De Steiger in Almere Haven. Now, they are the canvas for the Docks festival. Both young and established street art artists, local, national, and international, can leave their mark here with their graffiti art, every year in August. A new tradition in Almere.

77 Microhouse Slim Fit

Alseïdenstraat 2
ANA ROCHA Architecture
2016-2017

Slim Fit reinvigorates the concept of tiny housing. It is an award-winning design of the BouwEXPO Tiny Housing, organised by the municipality in 2016. This urban dwelling occupies no more than the area of two parked cars and has a vertical design with an elegant look. A separate living environment has been created on each four-by-four-metre floor. The kitchen is on the ground floor, where a wide decking in front of the sliding door extends the living area. Above that, the living unit with a large window, and on the top floor, a small window reveals the function of the bedroom and bathroom. Each floor can be closed off with a sliding door integrated in the stairwell. The use of wood contributes to a comfortable atmosphere. The interior is finished with birch plywood and the exterior with Ayous wood, placed vertically and affixed with countersunk screws. The concept focuses on small-scale living and densification. In this neighbourhood, with its playful, compact subdivision and small footprint, this works out very well. The diversity of the other Tiny Houses contributes to a special streetscape.

Smallest and Largest

On 22 May 2024, the local newspaper reported that this was the smallest house that was for sale. It has a surface area of 36 m² on a plot of 96 m². At the same time, the largest house in Almere, in Overgooi, was also for sale. This villa on Vijverbos 20 has a surface area of 919 m² on a plot of 2797 m². This enormous dwelling was built in 2009 and has 14 rooms, seven of which are bedrooms. It is a two-storey house with five bathrooms.

78 Ithaka

Poseidonsingel
VMX Architects
2011-2014
Don Murphy (proj.),
Ronald Rietveld (landscape.)

After winning a competition in 2007, concept developers Edwin Oostmeijer and André van Bekkum and VMX Architects were able to go ahead with project Ithaka. The aim was to make use of the diversity of residents to create a dynamic living environment. The result is a diverse collection of 135 residential units, ranging from 24 m² studios to 400 m² lofts. Ithaka combines urban qualities with a shared landscape. A U-shaped block encloses three sides of a collective park with a 1.1-hectare natural pond (Ronald Rietveld).

The ecological swimming pond consists of a rectangular concrete basin measuring 50 by 10 metres and 1.4 metres deep, surrounded by pond plants that purify the water. Below the jetty is the 'machine room' with pumps for circulation. On the fourth side, a moat forms the natural boundary of the plot.
Residential construction ranges from two to four storeys, with the occasional outlier to five, and back again. Each flat overlooks and has direct access to the centre's green space. The exterior of the buildings is characterised by abundant grout running out of the joints, the so-called 'beards'.

Sustainable

The botanical garden Ithaka was laid out after the houses were built here in 2011. The basic idea was a biotic environment. This means that it is not a planned garden with flowers and shrubs, but a landscape garden planted with indigenous wild herbs and plants. The oldest allotment garden association, 'Water-Land', has been based in Almere Haven since 1989. Some 350 gardeners are practising their hobby at VTV Water-Land here. The Association has the accreditation of

Natural Gardening, meaning that they contribute to greater biodiversity. The park includes an apiary, wildflower meadows, eco-walls, a bat house, and an amphibian pond.

79 Villa Homerus

Gigantenstraat
Hans Been, Johan van der Woude
2017-2018

Villa Homer is a true landmark at the edge of the Homerus neighbourhood. The building block was clad in light blue panels and surrounded by wavy balconies with white railings. The whole thing seems to swing. The secret is that the waves are different on each floor. Where the balcony protrudes further at the corner on one floor, it retreats again on the floor below. The waves on the side facades also do not run synchronously, and the windows and doors are placed slightly differently on each floor. The ground floor recedes and is clad in wood. That is where the storerooms are. The entrance in between is sober. The five storeys that follow contain five flats each. Layer six has three and the seventh floor contains two penthouses. The building block narrows there and ends with a cornice to echo the undulating balconies. The flats have underfloor heating and steel window frames in the facades. The views are of course splendid, with the Pampushout woods on one side, the gleaming IJmeer lake to the west and, at the foot, the many extraordinary villas built under own management in the Homerus neighbourhood.

Tiny Church

Almere Poort is also home to the only zero-energy church in the world. The wooden box with a slanted roof, designed by Edwin Vermeij, was realised at the Dettifosspad in 2016. The Tiny Church has a surface area of 50 m². The whole thing can be rotated so the solar panels on the roof always catch the sunlight. In 2022 a replica was built on the Floriade grounds, surrounded by a garden with sculptures by 12 artists, around the theme 'fruits of the mind'. These are virtues such as compassion, loyalty, and self-control.

The building functions as a church and meeting place, says initiator the reverent Pieter ter Veen. 'We mainly sit in a circle and engage in conversation with each other.'

80 FabricFacade

Zeussingel 41
CC-Studio, Studio TX
2011
Rob Veening (proj.)

The client, a visual artist, wanted a spacious, imaginative, and flexible house with vistas. At the same time, he wanted sufficient privacy and intimacy to retreat into his own world. This was achieved by stacking two interlocking L-shaped volumes, creating separate living and working zones. At the centre of the house is a void with a skylight. Together with the split-level floors, this provides the desired vistas and daylight penetrates deep into the house. This largely self-built house, popularly called the 'flap house', stands out because of its facade, which is clad in white strips. These Teflon and fibreglass strips are residual material from the food industry with a graphic pattern of air bubbles punched into them. According to building regulations, the houses in this neighbourhood had to be 'free-standing in a row', spaced five to ten centimetres apart to avoid noise nuisance. Although this standard was later abandoned, the gaps between this house and neighbouring properties are still visible. The rounded corners on the outside lend the house a soft profile.

Inntermezzo

The second owner, a 'care pianist', uses the ground floor for organising concerts he calls the Podium Poort series. The spacious mezzanine has meanwhile been converted to a B&B facility. The cladding of the house has also been applied to the garden house at the back of the plot, which is also a B&B. This part has an entrance on Dionysusstraat and is very popular with expats and tourists.

81 Heat Exchanger Station

Adriaen Blockstraat 7
Willem Schutter
2012

A structure made of aluminium sheets that were once bright red. Sun and light have dramatically toned down the colour so that it is now salmon-coloured. The rounded roofline makes the building look like an animal from a science fiction story, which at any moment might raise the trunk lying over its back to scan the blue sky with its spherical sensors. The whole thing is casually sprinkled with black specks of paint.
Behind the glass wall on the north side loom the boilers and pipes of the heat exchanger plant, which provides Almere Poort with district heating.

The hot water is a residual product of the power plant in Diemen and is pumped through an eight-kilometre-long transport pipeline through the IJ lake to be transferred to the district's grid at this Warmte Overdracht Station (WOS, heat exchanger station) through six heat exchangers. This, the largest WOS in the Netherlands, significantly reduces CO_2 emissions and supplies heat to 11,000 homes and businesses in a comfortable and eco-friendly way.

De Blocq van Kuffeler

In terms of water management this pumping station is the very core of life in the polder. In 1967, De Blocq van Kuffeler was the starting point of reclaiming an area of 43,000 hectares of land for agriculture, recreation, nature development, and housing. Four diesel engines pumped huge quantities of water off to the Markermeer. In a 2010 renovation, electric pumps were added. But, in case of a power blackout the old diesel engines can still come to the rescue of the polder residents.

82 Urban Villas Poortdreef

Poortdreef
Various architects
2022

In urban planning terms, Almere Poort has the shape of a fan, tapering towards the Hollandse Brug, where the train comes into the area. The long, straight Poortdreef forms the connection between this point and Oostvaardersdijk in the north. East of this wide avenue with a canal on either side, a strip is filled with city blocks. A building type midway between a villa and a flat. They line up neatly, in three rows thick, and are filled with rental and owner-occupied flats and some small business. The architecture shows that enormous variation is possible even within a clearly defined type and size, as evidenced by all the different balconies, colours, materials, and mouldings. These stout blocks of mostly four layers consolidate the urban vibe initiated with the coastal high-rise at Duin. The long row is broken by a prominent section of the Columbus quarter shopping centre designed by Erick van Egeraat. The lightning bolt line of the roof of this protruding section has a snow-white frame, which matches the main building transverse to it with its white wall surfaces.

No More

When Almere Poort was being developed in the late 1990s, Almere entered an ambitious phase. Generic building for always the same standard family gave way to DIY construction, diversity, urban density, and style. When Gerard Jan Hellinga started working for the city as an urban planner for Poort in 1997, mayor Ralph Pans welcomed him with the words: 'Just make sure we don't get more of this nothingness!'

83 Baitul Afiyat Mosque

Siliciumstraat 3-5
Farhan Alibux
2019

In the realisation of this pure central-plan building, the architect had an advisory role. His design was submitted to the members and to the head of the international religious community. After approval of the shell proposals, which were constructed by a contractor, experts from the community volunteered to work on the finishing. The fibreglass dome comes from Pakistan. It is pointed on the outside, but has a circular shape on the inside. The wreath of windows in the drum brings daylight into the large prayer room, which has a meditative character. The text 'Hearts find rest in the remembrance of Allah' illustrates the intention. The imam's residence occupies the strip at the back, where there is also a balcony. Minarets stand at the corners. In the centre of the front facade, a niche protrudes from the volume, crowned by a slender, tall tower, indicating the location of Mecca. All facades have concrete lesenes, with a tile pattern punched into them. The intervening spaces are filled with windows and brick slabs. The strong vertical articulation of the facades expresses growth and reaching upwards. At night, the mosque is illuminated in a mesmerising way.

Well-doing

Imam Safeer Siddiqui tells of a mother who walked past the mosque and told her little girl that it was a palace where princes and princesses lived. One passer-by, who was not from a Muslim background, upon seeing the building felt the urge to do something good. He donated money to the Humanity First Fund, a connected charity organisation. This 'house of peace and security' inspires people and brings them together, is the imam's experience. It is a place for prayer and meditation, and it also encourages people to contribute to the well-being of their fellow humans.

84 Achillesveld

Cascadepark
Hund Falk Architecten
2020

The project consists of a closely related group of 24 square detached houses, compact yet playfully grouped on a triangular point at the edge of Cascadepark. The donjon-like blocks of individual houses each have a rather closed character, although there is a playful brick element that enlivens the wall surfaces and a colourful window frame that marks the front door. A sunken roof terrace at the top of each unit forms an extra room, with a view of the vast park surrounding the buildings. The towers are close together and harmonise like houses in an organically grown village, but they also retain their privacy in this setting. The seven different types each have their own garden and parking, and of course have the surrounding park as an additional outdoor area. A black-and-white paved road connects all units and allows parking on site. Individual quality has been realised here in a high density setting with plenty of space all around. Achillesveld won the 2020 Almere Architecture Award.

Youth Team 'The Black Sheep', 1993

Football

Since 2023, Almere City FC represents the city in the Dutch Premier League. The club has a rich history, which started with the earlier 'Zwarte Schapen' (black sheep) from Amsterdam. In 1997 the name was changed to Sporting Flevoland, and meanwhile the Almere council was making plans to promote top sport in the city. This eventually led to the founding of FC Omniworld. An important step in the history of the club followed in the 2010/2011 season, when the name was changed once again, this time to Almere City FC.

85 Beach Town of the Randstad

Zeeduinweg a.e.
ZUS and various architects
2008-2030

Almere Duin is an ambitious area development that stems from the government's requirement for Almere to add 60,000 homes between 2010 and 2030. This expansion, known as the 'Schaalsprong' (scale leap), was to fulfil a significant part of the housing task in the northern wing of the Randstad area.
In 2008, the municipality of Almere organised a competition called 'Strandstad van de Randstad' (beach city of the Randstad) for a concept for an integrated area development of the western part of Almere Poort on the IJ lake.
The competition was held just before the financial crisis and concentrated on creating an area for living, working and recreation on the west side of the city, which had not been sketched out before. The urban plan of Duin, a collaboration between developer Amvest, the municipality of Almere and urban planning agencies BVR and ZUS, is special because of the order in which it was implemented: first the dune landscape was created, then the houses were built. For the landscape, almost two million cubic metres of sand were deposited to create dunes. Within this landscape, sand-coloured houses were scattered loosely or placed in small rows.
A wide boulevard forms the main artery of the area and runs along the coast on the waterfront. The design combines high and low densities, with tall residential towers along the coastal road offering wide views, taking full advantage of its location on the IJ lake. Beaches, dunes and forests alternate in the surrounding area. Forty years after the development of Almere Haven, the city rediscovered the potential of waterfront living, this time with a view of Amsterdam on the other side. If there is one city that represents the 'makeability' of the Netherlands and our entire engineering history, it is in Almere in Almere Duin. A freshwater dune landscape was created in a polder where once used to be a lake and before that a sea.

86 Kop Zuid I & Kop Zuid II

Zeeduinweg
Klunder Architecten
2017
Stefan Fremouw (proj.)

Kop Zuid I, an ensemble of four residential buildings called De Boei (57 flats), Catamaran (48 flats), Het Anker (26 flats), and Het Baken (59 flats), is freely arranged along the main road. They are finished in white, sand and brown brick colours, Duin's palette. The social rent, private-sector rent and owner-occupied flats differ in floor plans and the size of the balconies. The location at the edge of the district offers every resident a view of the IJ lake, with Amsterdam on the other side. It is the prelude to the larger-scale section known as Kop Zuid II. Kop Zuid II consists of San Francisco (84 flats), Valencia (58 flats), Sydney (107 flats), Kaapstad (88 flats), the Duinhal (7000 m² of commercial space) and Havana (68 flats). Together, they form the unique skyline of Almere Duin. San Francisco is a residential tower located in the lively heart of Duin. Its shell-white colour makes it one with the sparkle of the water and the clarity of the dune sand. Here you live spaciously, in a luxurious flat with a large terrace with sweeping views of the Randstad on the other side. Big-city living in a natural setting. Amid offices, shops, restaurants and a large supermarket, the motto 'Life on the beach' is fulfilled here.

Tower

The Citadel, the 'castle' that Christian de Portzamparc designed for Almere Stad 11 also has a tower. Shortly before the festive opening in 2006, it came to light that a conscientious civil servant had taken his own life. He had become convinced that the foundation of the tower was inferior and was at a loss as to how he could pass on this unnerving information to his superiors without creating a huge crisis. When everything was recalculated, his despair proved to be baseless. A sad story, indeed.

87 Zuiderduin I

Duinrugstraat
Groosman Architecten
2014-2017

The first housing project in Duin, designed by Groosman Architects, comprises over two hundred rental and owner-occupied houses, realised in Zuiderduin. This project stands out for its integration of landscape and spacious, bright homes. The houses are scattered among dunes, sometimes ten metres high, along winding roads surrounded by shell paths and marram grass. There are various housing types, including cubes, variants with extra floors and roof terraces, and some traditional houses with gabled roofs. By executing the facades in soft yellow/grey tones and using wood for the verandas, the architecture matches the colour palette of the dune landscape. Cars are parked in the owners' yards or in small car parks. The asphalt contains shells, contributing to the 'Beach City of the Randstad' slogan. The facades, executed in different sizes of brick, in a random bond, feature windows in various sizes and positions, which creates a playful effect.
The location of the houses creates attractive vistas and footpaths, overlooking the dune landscape.
On the Duinrugstraat, we see semi-detached houses interspersed with detached houses, resulting in a roomy streetscape. Duinvoetstraat showcases the concept of 'natural and urban' living, with spacious dwellings by the creek and the woods. This project illustrates how architecture and landscape can blend harmoniously.

Society queen

Society Queen Patty Brard certainly added some colour to Almere when she moved to the Duin neighbourhood. This lover of sun and beach states on her social media that she has found real peace and quiet in her new spot. Her detached beach house, characterised by sand, grey, and wood, gives her every opportunity to shine. When her move to 036 (Almere's area code) was made public, even the local second-hand stores placed racks of clothes with panther prints in their shop windows. For Patty, Almere is the Ibiza of the Netherlands.

88 Boomrijk

Noorderduinstraat
Van Bergen Kolpa
2015-2020

Scattered among spruce, beech and maple trees are 173 homes, ranging from single-family houses, semi-detached houses to detached villas. Van Bergen Kolpa purposefully adopted an approach that combined existing trees with the addition of new trees to create a lush and green character. Between semi-paved roads, lined with horizontal tree trunks, nature is very close by. Green wedges, wooded banks, wadis and meandering streams define the atmosphere. The single-family houses, detached villas and semi-detached houses blend into the woods of Duin. The materials and colour schemes of all the houses contribute to the natural character of the project. The roofs with ochre and brown tiles are reminiscent of autumn leaves and the facades of rugged tree bark. The yellow-framed windows continue in wooden slats, leading our gaze upwards. The steep roofs are intersected by robust chimneys at some houses. Paying attention to sustainability and the environment, the houses have been placed within the tree structure in such a way as to make best use of natural light, and sustainable materials have been used throughout. The central, green, public spaces are where the community comes together, contributing to a sense of belonging and connection.

Dendrology

Trees have lent their names to some neighbourhoods in Almere, such as Boomrijk. When the Japanese cherry trees blossom, people come from far and wide to the Regenboogbuurt 54. For many it has by now become a tradition to come and look at the more than 850 Japanese cherry trees. Their blossom supports and underlines the colour array of the architecture. Activities are organised under the blossoming trees and thousands of photos are taken of the pink splendour.

89 Arison Maritime Campus

Zeeduinweg 9
Paul de Ruiter
2018

At the Arison Maritime Academy and its associated CSMART Hotel, cruise ship personnel are (re-)trained and housed. The two buildings were designed to match architecturally, with the same structure and a transparent character. The complex is exclusively for Academy staff and guests.
The training centre features cutting-edge technologies such as engine rooms, simulators and ship bridges, grouped around a central hall with natural light via an immense skylight. Classrooms and staff rooms open onto this atrium, with balustrades and stairs panelled with light wooden slats.
The training centre's exterior is wide, while the 11-storey hotel with 176 rooms rises up into the sky.

Both buildings' facades are made of glass, five metres wide at the hotel and continuous from floor to ceiling, with aluminium cassettes in between. The wide cassettes are brown at the training centre, and yellow/white at the hotel, matching the dune palette.
The hotel rests on a plateau with a spacious entrance, reception, restaurant, gym and lounge. The cantilevered sun blinds reduce energy consumption through intelligent facades that respond to sunlight. Solar panels on the roof and insulation contribute to sustainability, a key design principle.

Checking Out

The famous song 'Hotel California' by The Eagles (1977) relates that although you can check out of the infamous hotel, 'you can never leave'. The Arison Hotel is beautiful, but only accessible to CSMART (Center for Simulator Maritime Training) invitees. So only they can enjoy the wonderful view.

90 Muiderburght

Marinaweg
ZZDP Architecten
2002
Peter de Clercq Zubli (proj.)

Three elegant residential towers with rounded corners and floating roofs. They are named after the three artificial islands south of Pampus: Drost, Warenar and Hooft. They are located at a prominent spot on the Almere coast, visible from Muiden and Amsterdam. The height of the towers rises to eleven storeys at the most inland volume. There are a total of 78 villa flats with curved indoor balconies, which, when viewed from a distance, lend a rhythmic, ascending articulation to the towers. Some units also have projecting triangular balconies. They add a playful touch to the smooth walls. Under the floating, cantilevered roofs are flats with sizes of up to 300 m^2. But the other units are also very spacious. The shell of pale yellow brick camouflages the internal concrete construction. Initially a solo project on this site, surrounded by woods full of foxes and rabbits, Muiderburght is now part of the highly urbanised coastal development Duin. Residents keep their expansive views of the marina at their feet, the rippling Marker lake, the white railway bridge in the distance and, of course, the famous Dutch skies all around them.

City and Fortress

Muiden may have the Muiderslot and the Groene Draak (Royal sailboat), but Almere has the Muiderburght. When the townspeople of Muiden objected against the construction of these elegant high-rises because they would violate their horizon, Almere felt it was also entitled to something Royal. The idea was to build a water palace before the coast of Poort, doing more justice to the Groene Draak. Fortunately, there was a change of course, because the ambition that had been formed has now become manifest in the high-rise area south of Muiderburght. The new and the old town really complement each other, also in terms of going out.

91 Museum Forest

Meesweg 7
Van Paridon x de Groot
2015-2017

In 2000, the Bosland foundation started creating a Museumbos (Museum Forest). A collection of forest rooms of one hectare each in the Cirkelbos between Waterlandseweg and Gooimeerdijk. Each room was filled in by an artist, who developed a concept for it. One such place is Tempo by Boto van der Meulen; a room where a lime tree is planted every year for a hundred years, each time with a bottle between its roots containing a message for the future. In Bos der Verandering (Forest of Change) by Ronald Buiting, shades of green will slowly be replaced by red ones. One of the most special places is Almere Boven. A thirty-metre-high hill, raised as a tribute to the 'Founding Fathers of Almere', the group of designers who defined Almere's character led by director Dirk Frieling. A path spirals around the hill to the top. There are benches by Sajoscha Talirz and a floor on which artist Gijs Frieling had a poem by his father placed. Those who climb all the way to the top are rewarded with views over the rustling treetops to the city silhouette in the distance. Next Architects' plan Circle Path has not been implemented, even though a path of that name circles along the rooms.

Plan

There is a plan.
I don't know the details.
So I can't tell you.
Exactly what or exactly where
or exactly who exactly when or
exactly how it will make sense.

But I do know this:
There is a plan
Now go and realize it.

Dirk Frieling

92 Oosterwold

Tureluurweg
MVRDV
2011-

Oosterwold, located in the district of Almere Hout, showcases the most recent area development in Almere. The area covers over 4300 hectares, originally agricultural land, and historically formed an agricultural enclave between Almere and Zeewolde. This development to the east acts as the rural counterpart to the urban developments in Almere Poort on the west side of the city.
New owners/residents have to prepare the farmland for construction themselves There is no underground infrastructure such as power lines and water mains. There is also no road network. This leads to a multitude of forms, variation in size and buildings that can be placed anywhere on the plot. The traditional grid has been abandoned, marking a break with conventional urban planning programmes. The firm MVRDV, led by Winy Maas, is responsible for this urbanism concept, developed in close cooperation with former councillor Adri Duivesteijn. Oosterwold, also called 'Freeland', is reminiscent of a 'free state' where private and collective activities are created with minimal interference from the government. Limits are set to ensure the rural character of the area is maintained: 18% construction, 8% roads, 13% public green, 2% water and 59% urban agriculture. Moreover, everyone in Oosterwold is personally responsible for energy supply, the different cycles and wastewater. Within this framework, individual creativity abounds. Since its launch in 2011, this has resulted in an organic multitude of forms, colours and materials. Yurts, houses built from sand-filled car tyres, minimalist bungalows, container houses, a revolving house, castle houses and tiny houses alternate with vineyards, sheep pastures, vegetable gardens, a bakery and a pizzeria, all bordered by green passages and colourful flower borders. In short, a truly varied cityscape.

93 Central Living Bosveld

Emile Durkheimweg 171
Bureau SLA
2017-2019
Peter van Assche, Nina Zurheide, Mathijs Cremers (proj.)

The Bosveld housing project, started in 2017 as Collective Private Commissioning, is an elongated, single-storey complex consisting of nine semi-detached bungalows, cutting across the landscape of Oosterwold. The building seems to float on its exactly one-metre-high, concrete beams, held together by bands of I-sections at the top and bottom. A long veranda with wide staircases provides access to both the front and back of the houses. The residents chose their own layout. The facades are made of glass sections and the entire complex is skirted by a slatted canopy. This wooden verge shields from bright sunlight. The floor, roof and partition walls between the houses are designed as hollow cassettes filled with insulating cellulose. The walls at the ends are panelled with horizontal slats, which harmonise with the continuous verge. The complex now has two other versions at different locations in Oosterwold 92. Each of these 'hamlets' is a hundred metres long, on plots of over 11,000 m². The houses range in size from 120 to 160 m². Combining modern architecture with sustainable construction techniques, this innovative project offers a unique living experience in a rural setting.

Divorce?

Researcher Ivan Nio did a sociological study into community building in Oosterwold.
One important finding: '... that the organic area development can lead to all sorts of conflicts, but that at the same time there is more community building than in the average new neighbourhood. In Oosterwold, individual motives are decisive but this does not stand in the way of a collective orientation.'

94 House in a House

Hannah Arendtweg 136
Bureau SLA
2019-2020

The clients wanted a detached house that would be bright, spacious and future-proof. Together with the architect, they arrived at a traditional house type with a gable roof and facades glazed along the entire length. The closed roof features a single skylight, which in turn forms the roof of a small greenhouse, the house within the house. Here, in the heart of the house, the plant collection flourishes and nature is literally brought inside. A guest room was set up on the upper floor. To make sure the house would be a lifetime home, the bedroom, bathroom and study had to be located on the ground floor. These were located on the garden side and these spaces merge seamlessly. The closed end walls have been elaborated into display cabinets, enclosing the glass facades. Parallel to an end wall is a simple kitchen unit, matching the functional kitchen. A long tree table sets the scene for shared meals and good conversations. On the outside, transverse supports give the house air, and with both a veranda on the entrance and garden facade, the living space is easily enlarged. The organically landscaped garden softens the hard lines of the house.

Vis à Vis

A theatre company that attracts a nationwide audience to Almere with spectacular, very inventive outdoor performances that always also address current issues. For instance, in *Silo 8*, a futuristic drama about care for the elderly. In 2007, Vis à Vis formed a connection with the city when it acquired a permanent performance space at Almeerderstrand. There, even the noisiest spectacles wouldn't disturb anyone. Everything looked fine, until more and more houses were built in the vicinity and the location came under scrutiny.

This type of performance is too loud to be held near people's houses. Will Almere provide a home port for his unique company?

95 A-frame House

Zonnelaan 2
La-di-da design & architecture
2020
Laura van Santen, Diederik de Koning (proj.)

Laura van Santen and Diederik de Koning of agency La-di-da have designed a series of private homes to develop a construction method that is both economically and ecologically sound. The A-frame house is one of four houses in this series, alongside Hietland in the Achterhoek region, the Dike house in Strijensas and the Tiny House in Deventer. The A-frame fits into the tradition of affordable construction. Instead of costly prefabricated walls, roofs and floors, the building was designed in such a way that all components could be easily assembled and lifted on site. As the roof is typically the most expensive element of a house, the architects decided on the A-frame model. The dimensions of the A-frame are based on the available length of SLS wood (Scandinavian Lumber Standard), which was used for the construction. The entire building is made of SLS wood, including the floor.
To minimise the use of environmentally problematic concrete, only the foundation is made of concrete. A wooden foundation would rot due to fluctuating groundwater levels. Thus, the designers combine economic efficiency with ecological stewardship.

Bio-based

La-di-da: 'An affordable bio-based cladding material has not yet been found; a whiff of cement was added to the wooden boards we use to make them more fire-resistant. Our next step is to look for a suitable alternative.'

96 Vliervelden

Goethelaan 163
KettingHuls
2020-2022

A central gateway forms the entrance to a farmyard, with a cowshed and hay barn on it. On either side, three residential buildings with 21 flats are built on the left and a shop and day-care centre on the right, respectively. The continuous, varied wooden facade is crowned with red roofs in different shapes. The residents have the farmers as neighbours and are surrounded by forty hectares of farmland.
The complex was inspired by pioneer barns in the United States, which had to house people, livestock and tools, and where verandas provided protection from wind and sun. The robust wooden facades with vertical accents are completed with openwork balustrades. The flats have very different floor plans. Porches, high ceilings and voids, and all with infinite views. The complex thus responds to the visual, anthroposophical design language of the barns.
Mountains had to be moved because of regulations on living in the yard, as this concept is unique in the Netherlands. Strict 'odour rules' were circumvented with a special regulation. Today, Vliervelden is considered a national prototype for building housing on farmland, offering livestock farmers new prospects.

Energetic

Tom and Tineke van den Berg run Almere's city farm. It covers 200 hectares in all, part of which lies near Vliervelden. They engage in biodynamic farming. This is a method that is not aiming for quick profit, but for maintaining the future quality of soil and water. A central building, inspired by traditional haystacks, is used to store straw. Next to it is a large stable/barn. There is a large store that sells biodynamic products and a comfortable place where people can sit and chat at one of the thick wooden tables made by artist Jos Bregman.

97 Swinging Art House

Friedrich Schillerhof
Jos Bregman, Ellen Winkel, Michel Post
2018-2020

A house with walls of straw bales in wooden caissons and a sprawling, swinging floor plan. A strip of meadow winds up from the garden to a tree-house situated above a green roof, offering a view over the fields of bio-dynamic farm Vliervelden 96, to which the house belongs. The ground-floor kitchen flows into a greenhouse and wild garden, where you descend to a sheltered spot by the reed-lined ditch. A spiral staircase then gives access to the treehouse again via the green roof. The connection with the surroundings is an essential feature of the design, which shows in the organic transition from the ground level to the green roof. Jos Bregman harvested most of the wood himself. He fitted beams, columns and planks with an ID chip, connected to a database, which records the origin. As an artist, Bregman has a deep respect for wood. He harvests it with reverence, gives each tree a name and in his treatments of it, brings to life all its qualities. He considers the applied wood in Swinging Art House as an imploded forest, part of his oeuvre as an artist.

Growing Music

The cowshed at De Vliervelden farm is very large. The cows are often in the meadows, so the barn can also be used to store equipment and organise various activities, such as music concerts. The Growing Music concerts and tours have found a permanent home here. The event calendar's central theme is 'growing green' and all theatre and music performances are related to that.

98 Rotating House

Toekomststraat
Joost Conijn
2023-2024

Approaching a house as a work of art rather than a dwelling – that is the concept of this cylindrical building. It consists of twelve panels placed on a circular concrete base. Half of the panels consist of curved glass, while the others are sealed and partly fitted with round window openings. The frame to which small steel wheels are attached is visible on the concrete base. With the mechanism of a bicycle, operated by human force, the forty-thousand-kilo house can be rotated to face the sun.
The idea that you can move a house on your own is at the heart of the design. No one had thought of this before, so artist and engineer Joost Conijn could only pursue his dream by just going for it. The exempted plots in Oosterwold 92 became his playground, where he started building and only afterwards checked whether the design complied with the applicable rules. This experiment reflects the character of Almere: innovative and bold. The project exemplifies Conijn's working method, in which he constantly explores the line between art and technology, humans and machines.

Free Spirits

For many years now, Almere has been attracting free spirits. Architects who wish to build their houses here without too much regulation, such as Conijn, and artists who find inspiration here. Sculptor and early Almerian Frans van der Ven designed seven so-called 'markers' for the archaeological site Zenit. They symbolised the fact that there was already fertile soil here 10,000 years ago.

99 Nobelhorst Estate

William Braggstraat 39
Scala Architecten
2016-2018
Mieke Bosse, Peter Drijver (proj.)

Scala Architects designed the urban plan for the Nobelhorst district, Almere's village, based on the theme 'Estate'. To anchor the concept in the neighbourhood and provide context for residents, a fictional genesis story for the Nobelhorst estate was written: the story of Hagobert. According to this story, Hagobert's old house disappeared in the waves of the Third Elizabeth flood (19 November 1424). The lords of Nobel, part of the entourage of Louis XIV, rebuilt the house in 1673.
The manor house, along with tenant houses and a toll house, is located at the end of a stately driveway, called Nobelstraat. Along this avenue are the 'Coach Houses', consisting of 16 rental houses and 13 owner-occupied houses.
The estate itself, located at the end of the Oprijlaan driveway, comprises 53 houses and 16 flats. The completely symmetrically arranged building has a raised principal floor as its base and is accessed via a grand staircase.
The central ressault is crowned with a classical pediment and the southern wings have a small extension. At the rear, there are several balconies and a balustrade on the guttering that runs all around, giving the building an elegant look.

Roundabout Art

The roundabout just in front of the Nobelhorst estate is just crying out for a work of art. Preparations to have this designed and executed by an Almerian artist are in full swing. The goal is to create a work of art that is not only aesthetically pleasing but also mirrors the unique identity and history of the estate. The chosen artwork will serve as a landmark, comparable to *Theatraal 2* by Frea Lenger from 2007 at Voorstraat. The work highlights the exit to Corrosia 60 where a related work hangs in the stairwell.

100 De Verwondering (The Wonderment)

Richard Feynmanstraat 7
ORGA architect
2021
Guus Degen (proj.)

The aim of primary school De Verwondering (wonderment) in Almere is to bring children in closer contact with nature by interweaving it with the built environment. The school has a special curriculum, but its physical environment has also been designed with this aim in mind, both the indoor and outdoor areas of the school building. Nature guided the spatial design of the school, inspired by the concept of natural habitats in which animal species coexist and thrive. In short, a biophilic school built from natural materials.
The school building has fourteen classrooms, divided into three clusters oriented in such a way that a large natural intermediate space is created for central, communal functions. This space, with abundant daylight, green walls and numerous flexible learning spaces, accommodates both large and small groups.
De Verwondering is also built 'of nature'. It is a hybrid timber building: the construction is partly CLT (Cross-Laminated Timber), partly timber-frame. The materials used for insulation, finishing, floors and furniture are all of bio-based origin. The use of natural materials and textures, combined with the green walls, stimulates both visual impressions and the sense of touch and smell. This creates a multi-sensory experience.

Quaaack!

Winner of the Gouden Kikker (Golden Frog) 2021.
'De Verwondering is an inspiring example of sustainable, social real estate at a very high level, in the broadest sense of the word. Not only because of the choice of natural materials, systems, and building methods, but also because of the design philosophy. The project is an inspiration to not only the students and staff of the school, but to the rest of the Netherlands as well.'

Index of names

This book is published in collaboration with Stichting Kunststad Almere.

And has been made possible with the generous support of Almere City Marketing, ArchiSienza | Fonds voor Architectuur en Wetenschap, Cultuurfonds Flevoland, Municipality of Almere, Marijke Jansen koRprodukties, nai010 publishers, Provincie Flevoland.

Texts
Ans van Berkum
Odette Breijinck

Translation
Jean Tee

Editorial advice
Paul Groenendijk
Marijke Jansen

Text editing
Leo Reijnen

Design
Koehorst in 't Veld
Bureau Sporken

Photography
Hans Jan Dürr
Geert van der Wijk

Additional illustrations
RIJP p. 4b, Odette Breijinck, p.8o, Topshot.nl, Vervaardiger: Rovorm, Collectie: Stadsarchief Almere, p.11o, Collectie Stadsarchief Almere p.15o, Collectie Stadsarchief Almere, p.20o, Collectie Stadsarchief Almere, p.25o, BDG architecten (render) p. 26b, Collectie Stadsarchief Almere, p.26o, Collectie Stadsarchief Almere, p.27o, Femke Kamps, p. 28o, Stadsarchief Almere p.30b, Stad & Natuur p. 34o, Ans van Berkum p. 37o, Collectie Stadsarchief Almere p. 44o, GAJ VBW Architecten p. 45o, Ed Sonneveld p. 46o, Roos Aldershoff p. 56, Collectie Stadsarchief Almere p. 60o, Hof van Almere p.63o, Cor Litjens p. 66o, Teo Krijgsman p, 67o, Feenstra Fotografie p. 69o, RSF Services p. 70o, Woonwerk (render) p. 71b, Collectie Stadsarchief Almere p. 71o, Liesbeth van der Pol p. 76o, Collectie Stadsarchief Almere p. 77o, Marijke Jansen p. 80o, Nico Nooij p. 83o, Collectie Stadsarchief Almere p. 84o, Pieter Kers |Beeld.nu p. 85o, Ans van Berkum p. 87, Collectie Stadsarchief Almere p. 90o, Collectie Stadsarchief Almere, Rovorm p.91b, Chris Soebroto p. 91o, Ans van Berkum p. 92o, J.U. Potuyt (RIJP) p. 93o, Topshot.nl, Vervaardiger: Rovorm, Collectie: Stadsarchief Almere p.94, Projectbureau Gouden Piramide p. 95o, Odette Breijinck p. 99, Collectie Stadsarchief Almere p. 103o, p. Mark Kirkenier p. 105o, Ans van Berkum p. 107o, Collectie Stadsarchief Almere p.109o, Collectie Stadsarchief Almere, Rovorm p. 115o, MVRDV | Daria Scagliola Brakkee, p. 117b, Collectie Stadsarchief Almere p. 119o, Jeannette Slütter p. 120o, Foodcoop Odin p. 121o, Murk Feitsma p.122o.

Printing
Grafistar

Publisher
Marcel Witvoet
nai010 publishers, Rotterdam

Production
Sara Duisters
nai010 publishers, Rotterdam

ISBN 978-94-6208-887-0

NUR 648
BISAC ARC024000

Also available in a Dutch edition
ISBN 978-94-6208-864-1

nai010 publishers is an internationally orientated publisher specialized in developing, producing and distributing books in the fields of architecture, urbanism, art and design. www.nai010.com

nai010 books are available internationally at selected bookstores and from the following distribution partners:

North, Central and South America - Artbook | D.A.P., New York, USA, dap@dapinc.com

Rest of the world - Idea Books, Amsterdam, the Netherlands, idea@ideabooks.nl

For general questions, please contact nai010 publishers directly at sales@nai010.com or visit our website www.nai010.com for further information